MW00440592

School
Reform
in Chicago

*Lessons in Policy
and Practice*

Edited by **Alexander Russo**

HARVARD EDUCATION PRESS

Library of Congress Control Number 2003115027
Paperback Edition: ISBN 1-891792-18-0
Library Edition: ISBN 1-891792-19-9

Published by Harvard Education Press,
an imprint of the Harvard Education Publishing Group

Harvard Education Press
8 Story Street
Cambridge, MA 02138

Cover Design: Alyssa Morris

The typefaces used in this book are Kuenstler 480 for the text and
Humanist 777 for display.

Contents

Foreword

Douglas Clayton

In 1988, the city of Chicago embarked on a historic effort to rebuild its failing school system. That ambitious and ongoing effort has attracted intense nationwide interest, particularly because many of the problems faced by Chicago's schools are shared by schools throughout the nation. As Chicago has implemented a series of bold, original reforms in the past 15 years, school systems throughout the United States have watched for clues as to how to solve their own chronic problems. For more than a decade, Chicago has richly deserved its reputation as a source and testing ground for school reform that other districts throughout America can learn from.

In the pages that follow, an impressive array of writers, scholars, teachers, administrators, and community and national activists describe and comment on the reforms that have come out of this sustained school reform effort. Lessons about the importance of community and parent involvement in schools; the need for school leaders who are committed to high-quality classroom instruction; the importance of investing in the professional development of teachers and principals; the value of essential partnerships among business, community, philanthropy, and government—lessons about these and other matters can be found in this book.

Of course, educational reform—like politics itself—always has local dimensions that are unique to particular schools or school systems. Chicago's efforts have been no exception to this rule: the city's reform measures have always been shaped to fit Chicago's distinctive circumstances. With that fact in mind, Alexander Russo and all of the other authors in this book have been careful to distinguish between what is unique to Chicago and what is common to many schools throughout the nation.

Special emphasis, however, is placed throughout the book on those reform measures that are relevant—and applicable—to other school systems. More than a history of recent school reforms in Chicago, this book is a practical, usable source of information and ideas for that great spectrum of people—teachers, administrators, policymakers, community activists, philanthropists, and so forth—that have a profound stake in ongoing school reform efforts throughout the United States.

It would be a mistake to view *School Reform in Chicago* first and foremost as a "history" of a particular time and place for a second reason as well: the reform efforts that the book describes are far from over. School reform—in Chicago, as in the nation as a whole—is still very much a work-in-progress, and this book is meant to serve and contribute to that urgent, continuing effort. Both as an account of past innovations and as an inspiration and guide for future reforms, *School Reform in Chicago* should prove an invaluable source of ideas and insights for school reformers throughout the country.

Introduction: "Third Wave"— or Lull—in Chicago School Reform?

Alexander Russo

When Paul Vallas, chief executive officer of the Chicago Public Schools (CPS), and Gery Chico, president of the city's Board of Education, departed in 2001, opinions were sharply divided about what would likely happen next for the Chicago schools. Some predicted that the exit of these two contentious figures would renew the city's flagging energy for change and signal the beginning of a "third wave" of school reform in Chicago. Others predicted that their successors would flop, becoming victims of leaner economic times, the deep and difficult challenges left to them, and the long shadows of the Vallas years.

Thus far, at least, neither prediction appears to be entirely true. Chicago schools don't seem to be experiencing a real renaissance, but nor are they falling apart. Certainly, there has been some notable progress—an increased focus on classroom instruction, an openness to new ideas, and an effort to refine some of the initiatives of the past. At the same time, there are many serious challenges that remain unmet and largely unaddressed—challenges such as significantly improving student achievement, reducing the high school dropout rate, and providing a clear direction for the future. Nearly three years into the post-Vallas era, it still remains to be seen whether this period will grow into something more or lapse into something less.

The following collection of essays and articles is far from comprehensive, but it does highlight some of the key issues and dynamics that have influenced school reform in Chicago, both during the Vallas years and thus far into the current administration. In doing so, it also identifies challenges and solutions that may be applicable to other large urban school systems. For example, former accountability czar Phil Hansen shares some of the lessons from Chicago's controversial school accountability and intervention initiatives. Ken Rolling, former head of the Chicago Annenberg Challenge, reflects on how privately funded school reform efforts can succeed if they overcome some chronic problems. Andrew Wade and Madeline Talbott show how parent and community involvement can support school improvement. And Richard Gelb describes what it's like to be in a school where new initiatives are often coming in waves that threaten to swamp the slow and difficult work of school-level improvement. Other pieces, some of which appeared in the *Harvard Education Letter* as part of its series, "Lessons from Chicago," highlight the struggle to improve instruction, teacher professional development, and more.

Chicago has long been a laboratory of school reform innovations in areas such as governance, leadership, accountability, and community involvement. Along the way there have been some notable successes, as well as many lessons learned. While the city is unique in some ways, these efforts are relevant to those being undertaken in other cities around the nation. And sharing those lessons is a large part of what this book is about.

DIFFERING EXPECTATIONS

A lot has happened since 1987, when U.S. Education Secretary William Bennett called Chicago's school system the worst in the nation. Even before the first wave of school reform legislation created local school councils (LSCs) in 1988, Chicago had a vibrant and multifaceted school reform community, elements of which advocated for what LSCs provided: more openness in the schools and a stronger role for parents and community members.

However, it was the shift in power from the dominant central bureaucracy on Pershing Road, where the Board of Education was then headquartered, to neighborhood stakeholders who could see with their own eyes the changes taking place in their local schools that sent a clear message to Chicago and the rest of the nation that this city was not afraid to try just about anything to improve its educational system. The LSCs—made up of parents, community members, and teachers—were a unique creation, all the more notable in a city where parents had often struggled for even the most minimal amount of openness or cooperation from the schools.

Still, the kind of academic success that parents, policymakers, and many school practitioners themselves wanted to see did not seem to take place until the second wave of school reform legislation in 1995, when control was consolidated again at the municipal level, but this time under the direct control of the mayor, Richard M. Daley. The 1995 law gave Mayor Daley direct authority over appointing the school board, allowed him to appoint a non-educator as chief executive officer of the city schools, and provided tremendous flexibility and power to the board in terms of funding, authority over individual schools, and dealings with the teachers union. Former city budget chief Paul Vallas was brought in as CEO to shake things up, get the school system running like a "real" business, and make sure that schools, students, teachers—even parents—were held accountable for how things went.

THE VALLAS YEARS

For better and for worse, Chicago schools underwent notable changes during the period when Paul Vallas and Gery Chico were in charge. By virtue of both the changes in state law and the leadership, the uncertainty that had often dominated the previous years was eased by a balanced budget and a stable, if combative, leadership team, as well as an end to the strikes that had hobbled progress and undercut public confidence.

There were downsides—poor implementation of too many programs, misconceived ideas about how to make schools work better, and a chronic underuse of the many school reform resources and community organizations that existed in the city. Local school councils barely survived the many challenges that they faced.

But, in a system where students had long been passed along from grade to grade regardless of what they were learning, Chicago's declaration of an "end" to social promotion dramatically changed the dynamics and incentives in its schools. The new probation and accountability system, while crude, created some sense of urgency and change. And innovations like small schools and charters took a small but strong foothold. By many measures, student achievement increased.

The fight over Chicago schools may not have been pleasant during those times, but nor was it boring. In some ways, the many conflicts helped keep school reform in Chicago alive because they challenged community groups and school reform organizations to stay in the fight.

LIFE AFTER VALLAS

According to those who predicted a third wave of school reform when Vallas left, this would be a golden era in which the local school councils, community groups, reformers, and philanthropies would all work more closely with the school system to focus on instruction and learning. Those who had been frozen out could add their voices, damage could be undone, and long-needed changes to the system could finally be addressed in areas like professional development, recruitment and retention, and revamping neighborhood high schools.

And yet, there was also some cause for pessimism. By the time Vallas left in 2001, the economy was already hurting and many of the "easy" fixes had been adopted—building schools, moving out of Pershing Road, getting the buses to run on time, setting up a summer school program. At the same time, it seemed unlikely that anyone could match Vallas' force of personality and twisted charisma, which seemed to galvanize both his opponents and supporters. The fact that the increasingly impatient mayor had hired someone who was neither politically experienced nor deeply knowledgeable about education as Vallas' successor only seemed to confirm this initial pessimism.

A THIRD WAVE?

Truth be told, progress had already been slowing down during the last year or two while Vallas and Chico were at the helm. Just as the seeds of progress during the Vallas years were sown before he arrived, so too were the seeds of progress for the current period being sown while Vallas was still in office. To some extent, the changing of the guard in 2001 helped move things along, promoted progress, and ushered in new ideas that were waiting in the wings. And, true enough, there has been some rejuvenation and progress during the past couple of years. There are many new faces both inside the system and among the reform groups, several new initiatives and policies, a certain amount of academic progress, and—perhaps most notably—a clear change of approach by the top leaders.

In general, the mood among the various stakeholders has been calmer, more cooperative, and less confrontational. While younger and less experienced than Vallas, current schools CEO Arne Duncan is equally earnest in his desire to see children do better and is much less unnecessarily combative. Among educators and reformers alike there is some sense of finally being able to get down to the business of improving teaching and learning in the classroom.

Those who point to the progress and accomplishments of the current team often emphasize the unusual, publicly shared leadership that exists between Duncan and career educator Barbara Eason-Watkins, his chief education officer. Playing a much stronger role than her nominal predecessor, Eason-Watkins is a veteran principal of an extremely successful school in one of Chicago's poorest neighborhoods. Together, Eason-Watkins and Duncan have shared the heavy load of leading the Chicago school system and developed a number of new ideas and approaches that are focused on instructional issues rather than accountability.

The teamwork between Duncan and Board of Education president Michael Scott has also been fruitful. As a long-time political player in Chicago with strong connections to the West Side, Scott is ideally suited to handle the tough politics that come up all the time, and he largely leaves policy issues to Duncan rather than getting involved with his own programs. During extremely tight fiscal times, the pair have thus far fought off major budget cuts from the state, and even restored funding to the district's capital campaign program.

The new team's accomplishments are several. They have brought in a number of experienced reformers and private-sector gurus. They have reorganized from six massive subdistricts into 24 smaller areas. They have funded school-based reading specialists to help classroom teachers implement more effective reading programs. And they have kept up the drumbeat that Chicago schools are on the move but still need improvement.

Perhaps most important, there have been no major scandals and no marked or immediate falloff in student achievement from the previous administration. Duncan closed three low-performing schools during the spring of his first year at the helm. He oversaw the development of a much-needed new accountability rating system for schools that measures progress as well as absolute achievement. In 2003, he removed another handful of principals from their positions for chronic academic failure. The student retention program remains largely in place.

At the same time, there seems to be increased openness at the Board of Education, especially in regard to community and school reform groups who had been frozen out for many years. To some extent, the long-insular Chicago school system is being opened up to outside ideas and reforms, whether they come from one of Chicago's many school reform groups or from another part of the country.

The Duncan team has also been open to increasing the various kinds of charters and small schools.

A LULL?

Despite these accomplishments, however, there are several areas where things do not seem to have progressed as well or as far as needed. They fall into the category of gaffes and missed opportunities rather than outright flops, but they are cause for concern nonetheless. It could also be said that at least some of the energy around school reform has diminished somewhat since Vallas et al. departed, and that recent progress has already been too slow in coming for the current team.

Most problematic of all may be the large and growing number of policy initiatives, a tendency toward proliferation that was part of the demise of Vallas and is a danger in any school leadership situation. Already, the Duncan team has initiated its own set of major new programs—the human capital initiative, the education initiative, the district reorganization, and the reading initiative.

Each program makes sense to some extent individually, but together they threaten to dilute reform or cause confusion and resistance. The new "education initiative," unveiled with great ceremony in 2002, has already become somewhat of an afterthought. For example, the ideas and information collected as part of the professional development audit in 2002 do not seem to have had much follow through.

Even the site-based coaching initiative, which initially focused narrowly on reading in the elementary grades, has been massively expanded to high schools and to other disciplines. Duncan and his team are spending millions on school-based reading, math, and science coaches without a well-designed program or clear evidence of success.

More important, the Duncan initiatives have not yet yielded any standout accomplishments or generated a strong sense of energy or momentum. Whether or not the teachers go on strike, these conflicts distract from making changes. The programs and policies that have been unveiled since 2001 don't include anything powerful or compelling enough to take Chicago schools another large step forward. Well-crafted or not, they seem too small to effect widespread, obvious change. By and large, Chicago no longer seems to be at the forefront of big-city school reform.

At the same time, Duncan's team apparently has not followed up on clear opportunities to make further progress. Duncan followed his most notable and controversial first-year accomplishment—closing three persistently failing schools—with a more cautious approach in year two. He helped push through legislation that at least symbolically restored some of teachers' lost bargaining rights, and then negotiated a contract with the teachers union that contains seemingly few substantive changes in how teachers are evaluated, assigned, or trained. And he has generally approached No Child Left Behind defensively, rather than using it as an opportunity to push for further change.

In taking these steps, Duncan has reduced conflict and created new opportunities, but he also appeared to lose whatever capacity he initially had to put pressure on the system. That no one fears Duncan as much as Vallas is not necessarily a bad thing. But in big-city school systems and highly political environments like Chicago, there is a fine line between a lack of fear and a lack of respect.

There are several other obstacles in the way. Even as Duncan continues to centralize programs, he and his team have yet to deal with the local school councils that can help make or break his efforts. Thus far he has avoided confronting them directly—a wise move, perhaps, given Vallas' experience—and has quietly continued to diminish their control over school budgets. But it is hard to imagine how Duncan and his team can make even further changes without either enlisting or bypassing the LSCs.

WHAT'S NEXT?

Looking to the future, Chicago schools face a combination of challenges, new and old. Certainly, the challenge of raising student achievement to more reasonable levels has not diminished. State and local test scores showed mixed progress last year. The dropout rate remains high and disproportionately affects blacks and Latinos, and more than half of the city's schools are not making adequate progress under federal guidelines. A recently released report on compensatory education in Chicago claimed that the district still focuses more of its efforts and resources on elite and magnet schools rather than on troubled neighborhood schools.

Nor has the challenge of making the public system a viable competitor to suburban and private schools been overcome. Despite all the new buildings and fancy new programs, newspaper reports from last summer suggested that just as many parents were taking their children out of the Chicago public schools for private or suburban alternatives as before 1995, the year the mayor took over.

And the challenges are not likely to get any easier in the short run. Perhaps the most prominent of the newer challenges will be what to do about the No Child Left Behind Act. Thus far the reaction has often been defensive and dismissive—an ironic response, given that increased federal funding has helped Chicago schools avoid serious cuts and that the main focus of the law, increased achievement for poor and minority children, is theoretically nothing new here.

And yet, Duncan et al. seem to have been hoping that NCLB will go away, or they stubbornly state that CPS already does whatever the act requires, in its own way. The main advantage of NCLB is that it has provided an easy scapegoat—a new enemy for CPS and City Hall and even the reform groups to rail against, instead of fighting among themselves.

But at some point the Duncan team will have to use NCLB for a more constructive purpose: to push for more change. Otherwise, without more concrete signs of progress, it seems inevitable that the mayor will once again start complaining, suggesting his own initiatives, and ultimately searching for a replacement for Duncan—just as he did with Vallas. The talk about who will replace Duncan started within months of his arrival and never seems far off.

Still, both outcomes seem equally possible. It remains to be seen whether this will turn into a third wave or merely a lull—an intermission or consolidation period that will soon demand another change and another big push forward. It may be too soon to tell, but the issue bears consideration and offers an important lens through which to view both the current effort at school reform in Chicago and the one that preceded it.

PART I

Schools and Community

1

The Power—and Limits— of Civic Capacity

Alexander Russo

I n 2002, the Chicago Public Schools (CPS) rolled out a new principal assessment program aimed at giving principals detailed and ongoing feedback on their performance. The program, called EXCEL, replaces the traditional one-shot annual evaluation form that has been used for years. It is just one of several major new programs unveiled in Chicago for the 2002–2003 school year, and far from the largest.

But what makes EXCEL notable is that—like many efforts here—it was developed with the help of one of Chicago's many education groups that serve as partners in the reform effort. EXCEL was an initiative of Leaders for Quality Education (LQE), a group organized by the city's business community, and the Chicago Principals and Administrators Association. The Chicago-based MacArthur Foundation and others provided funding.

Chicago may not have as many charter schools or big-name education leaders as other major cities, but perhaps no other school system in the nation is as influenced by such a vast array of businesses, philanthropies, universities, and community groups. These groups come in all shapes and sizes, and get involved in schools in nearly every way imaginable. Some are brought in by teachers and parents, some through district initiatives, and others through local school leaders, principals, and policymakers.

These groups aren't just business-supported organizations like LQE. Some, like the Golden Apple Foundation, provide important support to teachers to acquire books and supplies. Community groups such as West Town United work mostly with parents on education and governance issues. Others, like the Chicago Arts Partnership in Education (CAPE), help teachers improve classroom instruction. Advocacy and research groups such as Designs for Change work on a panoply of fronts.

Of course, Chicago schools weren't always this open to outside influences. After a long history of being seen as a fortress closed to parents and outside organizations, and with little university involvement, the Chicago schools were dramatically opened up in 1988 with the creation of elected local school councils (LSCs) at every school. These relationships have transformed the way Chicago's education policy is made and carried out.

The creation of LSCs gave schools control over discretionary dollars, which allowed them to seek (or refuse) services from any number of different types of groups and contract directly with them, rather than go through the district office. After 1995, the accountability system under Chicago schools CEO Paul Vallas began requiring that low-performing schools have "external partners" and intervention specialists, who often came from nearby schools of education.

According to some experts, these changes and activities are the result of, as much as the cause of, a tremendous amount of "civic capacity" in Chicago, which in turn has helped drive the school system toward academic reform. "The local community has to come together around what they want their schools to be," says Dorothy Shipps of Columbia University's Teachers College. "Chicago has this incredibly well-organized business community [and] a very strong community-based set of organizations." In her research, Shipps argues that legislative and educational reforms follow civic capacity. She holds that the 1988 decentralization and the 1995 mayoral takeover of the Chicago schools were largely prompted by these outside groups, rather than by the school system itself, and that reform has been fundamentally shaped by Chicago's civic organizations.

Such influence was demonstrated between 1995 and 2000, when the Chicago Annenberg Challenge spent $50 million to develop numerous networks providing support to schools, and had an especially strong impact on 16 "breakthrough" schools. Business and other groups have been involved in creating PENCIL, a principal recruitment initiative that helps local schools screen candidates, and the district-supported Principal Assessment Center, where principal candidates can go through real-world simulations of a typical day's decisions and emergencies. Similarly, the corporate-civic group Chicago United worked to interest teachers in applying for National Board certification.

A MIXED BLESSING

Not every collaboration goes smoothly or successfully, of course, nor is there always agreement about how much credit —or blame—the groups are due for their efforts. Some schools have resisted the "intrusion" of outside groups into decision-making and building politics. Staffing problems and personal dynamics undermined a massive collaborative effort to improve professional development for teachers at troubled Manley High School, despite substantial planning and funding among several groups, according to the school reform magazine *Catalyst*.

The multitude of initiatives can itself create problems, according to education researcher John Easton of the Consortium on Chicago School Research. "It's a good thing as long as the market works and the bad [programs] are filtered to the bottom and the good ones to the top," says Easton. "I don't think it's as efficient a market as it could be, however. Some of the losers are still on the market." A 1994 Consortium report warned of schools becoming "Christmas trees," with as many as 20 different initiatives taking place at the same time.

Confusion among multiple reform efforts has been a widespread problem since early in the reform era, says Don Moore, executive director of the research and advocacy organization Designs for Change. The problem got worse after 1995, he says, when "the central office initiated too many programs" and created an additional layer of probation managers, external partners, and literacy specialists whose efforts were not always integrated. "There's a real need to help principals and local school councils understand that they need to develop a coherent instructional strategy," says Moore.

According to John Easton, the most successful schools are those that figure out how to adapt a district- or group-sponsored initiative into something that makes sense for the individual school. These schools, Easton says, are able to garner additional resources for their schools and implement new efforts effectively. Many of these schools "already know what they want," says Easton, and are simply trying to find ways to get help implementing their vision. "They're not looking to an outside organization to tell them what kind of reading program they should have."

THE POLITICS OF PARTNERSHIP

The increasingly close interactions with the school system have created special challenges for outside groups, too, especially their ability to function as independent external critics. For example, several researchers involved in the Consortium on Chicago School Research, which bills itself as "an independent federation of Chicago area organizations that conducts research on ways to improve Chicago's public schools," have gone to work for CPS in recent years or have worked simultaneously for both organizations.

For Chicago, where the outside groups and the inside officials have long kept their distance, the changed relationships are noteworthy. While few criticize the new leadership for bringing in as much talent as it can, the new allegiances and the increased funding from central budgets raise questions about how much careful scrutiny the groups can provide, especially when they are working with CPS under contract.

Some insiders speculate that the external-partner program has been maintained for political reasons despite long-standing questions about its effectiveness. The program provides more than $5 million to roughly 20 outside groups each year. Others question whether local universities and the Consortium can provide objective research on reform effects while having close financial relationships with the district. Easton, who for a period split time between the Consortium and the district, says, "We continue to be as vigilant as we can," adding that he viewed his job at CPS as that of a "technical advisor" without the political interests or risks of a CPS insider.

Related or not, one surprising problem is that, for all of the research capacity in the city, conclusive information on the impact of specific initiatives remains surprisingly hard to come by. School- and program-specific results are more likely to come from a news outlet or a mandated disclosure of information by the state. In contrast, research published by the Consortium and others often masks the names of individual schools and outside groups that are involved. District-sponsored collaborations such as the external partner program have also gone unmeasured in terms of comparing and publishing results, despite millions of dollars spent.

Overall, however, most in Chicago agree that having such a broad array of groups creates more benefits than drawbacks. For example, Kinzie Elementary School principal Mary Palermo cites her school's long and successful track record working with universities, community groups, and non-profits, including coordinating staff development programs with nearby St. Xavier University and a character education curriculum through Chicago Communities in Schools. "The question I always ask is, 'What can we get out of this?'" she says. "I'm involved with all sorts of partnerships, and they have been very successful here," she says about her school, located on the city's Southwest Side.

When partnerships work well, they can give schools more than the obvious material benefits: they can also be morale building, as schools share responsibility for improvement with community, business, and research groups. "Any time you get these groups working with teachers, [teachers] don't feel as alone and isolated," says Principal Jim Cosme of Otis Elementary School. At a time when school practitioners are saddled with much blame and little credit for how reforms fare, that is a generous gift indeed.

This article originally appeared in the Harvard Education Letter *(January/February 2003).*

FOR FURTHER INFORMATION

L. Duffrin. "Seen as a Model, Manley Plan Falls Short." *Catalyst* (June 2002). Available online at www.catalyst-chicago.org/06-02/0602main1.htm

P.A. Sebring, A.S. Bryk, J.Q. Easton, et al. *Charting Reform: Chicago Teachers Take Stock*. Chicago: Consortium on Chicago School Research, 1995.

D. Shipps. "The Businessman's Educator: Mayoral Takeover and Non-Traditional Leadership in Chicago." In L. Cuban and M. Usdan, eds., *Powerful Reforms with Shallow Roots: Improving America's Urban Schools*. New York: Teachers College Press, 2002.

2

Reflections on the Chicago Annenberg Challenge

Ken Rolling

Ken Rolling directed the Chicago Annenberg Challenge for its six-year run. Prior to directing the Challenge, he spent ten years at the Woods Fund of Chicago as program officer for its community organizing and school reform programs.

For six years, from 1995 through 2001, the Chicago Annenberg Challenge—one of 18 Annenberg sites around the country—was the largest privately funded school reform project in the city, providing almost $54 million in new funds for the Chicago Public Schools (CPS).

During that time, the Challenge—along with the rest of the Chicago funding community—learned several important lessons about funders' roles in supporting and participating in school reform. We learned lessons about better and best approaches to improving educational opportunities for students

23

and teachers alike. We burned our fingers in the political fires of school reform. We struggled to make meaning of school reform efforts that were entirely new. We learned about the complexities of improving educational opportunities in a diverse urban school system.

As one of our board members remarked early on, "We have much to be humble about." And even to this day it is not clear that the lessons have been completely taken to heart and implemented. But that may only be an indication of the difficulty we continue to face as funders, school reformers, and some combination of the two.

The experience of the Challenge was in many ways not a new one. Private funders have played a central role in Chicago school reform for the past 20 years, during which time they not only provided generous and consistent support for improvements in Chicago's public schools, but also shaped the course of school reform by their grant decisions and by their engagement (or lack thereof) in the decisions that drive school reform. All told, more than 30 Chicago-area funders were responsible for the Chicago Challenge's meeting its matching funding requirements of $100 million.

In Chicago and elsewhere, the fundamental quandary for funders is whether they are solely financial supporters of others' work or whether they are reformers—doers of reform—themselves. Funders have difficulty sorting out their roles and actions and, consequently, send mixed messages about their good intentions by only partially engaging in the messy work of school reform. They want their stamp placed clearly on successful programs, but prefer to avoid the controversy involved in taking on the system of public education in their district and, indeed, in the country as a whole. Fear of recriminations from the IRS—that is, the loss of favorable tax status if they are perceived as engaging in political action—is one real cloud hanging over funding decisions.

More often, however, it is concern about appearing to rock the boat that keeps funders from challenging the direction of school reform. Many foundation trustees wanted to collaborate with CPS administrators and support their efforts, rather than challenge them on the best way to improve schools. Even when schools chief Paul Vallas became insulting and dismissive, we grumbled and complained in private but did not confront him publicly or engage in the public discourse raging at that time about the direction of Chicago school reform.

Funders are caught in (but hesitate to publicly engage in) partisan political fights over power and control of the direction of school reform in our school districts. Some years ago, when I was working for the Woods Fund of Chicago, a new trustee who was sitting through a discussion of Chicago school reform with active school reformers whispered to me, "Good God. It's all about power and not about the kids and their education!" An accurate description of much public discourse about school reform in this country, for sure.

However, failing to engage in politically charged debates over the direction of school reform relegates funders to supporting specific, limited programs that affect few students and prevents funders from looking comprehensively at the issues and needs of public education for all students—the ultimate goal of school reform. Individual funders also often wish to maintain their independence and come up with their own ideas for how to support school reform.

There are at least 100 discrete, individually funded programs supported in the Chicago Public Schools, some of them affecting a few classes, some a few schools, some a particular curriculum (e.g., financial education). But most programs are not connected to systemic reform. Some schools have as many as 25 different outside programs operating in their school buildings at the same time. But individual, unconnected programs don't add up to improved schools. Most of our attempts in the Challenge to coordinate and streamline these programs were unsuccessful.

Another widespread problem we faced is that private funders too easily gave into a business-and-market model of school reform, accepting numeric, quantifiable outcomes based on standardized tests as the criteria for academic success. In hindsight, it seems clear that we could have mounted a communications effort to expose the misuse of test scores as indicators of the success and failure of our schools and students.

A major and early mistake in the Chicago Annenberg Challenge was our initial decision against developing a vibrant communications program. At a meeting of the Challenge board of directors in early fall 1995, just as the Challenge was getting under way, we decided against mounting a communications program, believing the Challenge should keep its head down until we had something—specific success stories—to tell the world. We lost precious ground in the political wars over the direction of Chicago school reform and missed valuable opportunities to communicate what we were learning. The Chicago school reform "miracle" was thus determined by the Chicago Public Schools' focus on accountability and threats, rather than by teaching and learning efforts taking place in Chicago's neighborhood schools.

Last but not least, we funders pour a disproportionate amount of funds into research that does not connect with practice. The Chicago Challenge raised $3.5 million in research funds to support the largest urban-based school reform research project in the country, the Chicago Annenberg Research Project (CARP). But we didn't break through the barrier that exists between research as the preserve of our universities and practice at the public school level. The research was neither timely nor ever complete enough to influence our work. Support provided for CARP turned out to be general support for the organization of researchers and educational experts with whom we had contracted.

However, the silver lining is how well used that research has been by the current CPS administration team. In effect, we laid the groundwork for what is now referred to as the "third wave" of school reform in Chicago.

While the Chicago Annenberg Challenge provides a lens through which sometimes difficult experiences of funders and funder/reformers can be translated into lessons learned, the several contributions of the Challenge are lessons learned as well. The Challenge grew out of, continued, and pushed forward the Chicago "big-tent" approach to school reform, broadening and deepening public engagement in public schools. During its six-year run, the Chicago Annenberg Challenge was the single largest supporter of professional development for CPS teachers. The Challenge created teaching and learning partnerships that connected more than 200 local schools with outside partners, and it created the Chicago Public Education

Fund. The Challenge left in place at least 20 organizations whose capacity and ability to work substantively with schools was built with Challenge funds and direction. The findings of the Chicago Annenberg Research Project, with its focus on how all children can and do learn when academically challenged, and on how teaching content and methods matter for every child in every classroom, continue to have an impact on school reform in Chicago and far beyond Chicago's borders.

In the greater circle of Chicago-based funders today, we find more focused, collaborative school reform efforts, some worked out in conjunction with the new, more open administration of CEO Arne Duncan. In addition, funders are working together on high school reform initiatives and new community schools programs.

When all is said and done, the Chicago Annenberg Challenge and Chicago's funding community do have "much to be humble about." These lessons—and these accomplishments by the Chicago Annenberg Challenge—will remain an integral part of Chicago school reform as lessons learned are put into practice.

3

Site-Based Management During a Time of Centralization

Andrew G. Wade

Andrew G. Wade, founder and executive director of one of Chicago's newest school reform and advocacy organizations, the Chicago School Leadership Cooperative, has been involved in school reform in Chicago for over a decade. In recent years the Cooperative has become an instrumental player on issues affecting local school councils.

Over the past eight years, two very different visions of school reform have been operating in Chicago—sometimes in direct conflict and sometimes with something approaching cooperation. One vision has its roots in the leadership of Mayor Harold Washington, during whose tenure (1983–1987) a popular victory over entrenched bureaucratic interests took place. The 1988 school reform law that resulted from these efforts created powerful elected councils at every Chicago public school, giving a new voice to communities and parents that had long been shut out of the school reform process.

The other vision, which began in 1995 with the arrival of schools CEO Paul Vallas and the mayor's takeover of the school system and which continues to the present, has focused on a very different set of priorities, including accountability to tough standards for school improvement and the expansion of programs and facilities under the direction of the central office.

The result of these different visions is a patchwork of school reform laws that in effect have divided control over the schools between two sites of authority—the central office and the local school councils (LSCs).

WHAT ARE THE LSCS?

Now 15 years old, Chicago's LSCs comprise the largest concentration of non-white, female, and economically disadvantaged elected officials in the nation. Since the first citywide LSC elections were held in 1989, literally tens of thousands of Chicagoans have served on Chicago's 590 councils, which govern the vast majority of schools in the city.

Each council includes the school principal, six parents, and two community members elected by adults living within the school attendance area, as well as two teacher representatives and (in high schools) an elected student representative.

Unlike site councils in other cities, Chicago's LSCs are invested with considerable decisionmaking authority. Their most unique feature is the power to award a four-year performance contract to the school principal. In addition, councils have approval power over the local discretionary budget and school improvement plans. LSCs also traditionally play a role in bringing in community resources and advocating for local school interests in the central administration and at other levels of government.

WHAT DOES THE RESEARCH SAY?

In general, research supports the basic hypothesis of the 1988 reform—that democratic localism is a viable lever for school change. Research conducted by the Chicago Consortium on School Research shows that, as early as 1993, evidence of meaningful restructuring could be found in about half of low-performing elementary schools, with another 25 percent taking steps in the right direction. Schools with a strong democracy and balanced LSC governance appeared to make the most strides. In 1997, the Consortium reported that "the vast majority of LSCs are viable governance organizations that responsibly carry out their mandated duties and are active in building school and community partnerships. The initial worries that councils would infringe upon professional autonomy have proved unfounded."

And yet, it would be an overstatement to call decentralization a ringing success—a "work in progress" would be more apt. Most schools moved ahead under local control, but many did not, especially at the secondary level. While the stereotype of conflict-laden LSCs was overblown, 12 percent of LSC members identified conflict as a problem. More common is the problem of ennui, with low participation in biannual LSC elections, inadequate training, minimal working structures, and/or co-optation by principals who hand picked or simply ignored their councils.

Contrary to what many may think, LSCs have never been well supported financially. For example, neither the 1988 nor the 1995 reform law allocated funds to implement the LSC system. Private funding for LSC recruitment and training dropped significantly after the first LSC election, and has been subject to the vicissitudes of funding trends and the economy ever since. And obstruction or unresponsiveness from the central administration has been a consistent challenge, although there has been some improvement within the last two years.

HOW LSCS FARED, 1995–2001

When the Vallas administration came into power in 1995, many LSC leaders were hopeful that the energy of the new leader would translate into systemic change and support for their local work.

Such optimism did not last long.

Vallas and the LSCs did enjoy a brief honeymoon through the LSC elections in spring 1996, which saw a modest rise in LSC participation. Yet suspicions of the new administration grew steadily in the wake of what LSC members saw as direct infringements on their local prerogative. Among many examples, Vallas froze state antipoverty funds, the primary source of dollars controlled by local schools, at their 1995 levels—effectively reducing LSC control over school budgets from roughly 50 percent to 36 percent of the total Chicago Public Schools (CPS) budget. Vallas also established probation, remediation, and reconstitution policies that superseded LSC authority.

Perhaps most significantly, the central administration also won control over training the LSCs. As a result, many of the community-based and school reform organizations that had been the most consistent source of support for LSCs found it significantly more difficult to gain access to the constituencies they served. Reform groups that dared to criticize the administration found themselves branded as self-interested parties seeking to siphon funding away from schools and children.

The conflict between the two reform traditions reached a boiling point in 1999, when Vallas proposed Senate Bill (SB) 652, which would give him veto power over principal selection and essentially eliminate LSCs as meaningful decision-makers. His effort failed, though the watered-down final version of the proposal did require LSC members to undergo criminal background checks, a move many low-income and minority LSC members felt as a racist slight.

Ironically, the effort to eliminate LSCs did much to revitalize them. The following year the foundation community poured significant new funding into community outreach for the LSC election, wisely anticipating that LSC members not initiated in the curious art of Springfield compromise would not recognize the watered-down SB 652 as a major victory for Vallas. Shortly after the LSC election, over 50 LSC leaders, community groups, education organizations, and elected officials worked collaboratively to reverse the policy that barred community groups from providing basic LSC training.

While the Vallas administration continued to spar with LSCs and their supporters until the very end, SB 652 produced a stalemate between the two reform traditions that fundamentally shifted the politics of Chicago school reform. Many key players from both reform traditions recognized this stalemate and began seeking new ways to rebuild relationships in order to move the overall reform agenda forward. Disagreements about what that agenda should be continued, but in an environment that reflected the growing recognition of the need to work together. The politics of confrontation had given way to the politics of collaboration.

WHERE LSCS STAND TODAY

Sadly, the philosophical battles of the late 1990s distracted attention from the overall purpose of school reform: to improve the quality of schools. Both reform wings can lay claim to some meaningful accomplishments and must accept responsibilities for some failures. While current Board of Education president Michael Scott and chief executive Arne Duncan made mending fences an early priority upon their arrival in 2001, two years later their stance on LSCs remains difficult to pin down.

On the one hand, many LSC supporters once castigated as a "cottage industry" were invited to share their ideas. Both wings of school reform have enthusiastically endorsed the new administration's priority of improving classroom instruction and have shifted their program emphases accordingly.

On the other hand, efforts to build a strong alliance between the new administration and LSCs have not yet borne much fruit. LSCs continue to be plagued by a shortage of high-quality training, inconsistent information, and policy decisions that marginalize or ignore their concerns. While the new administration has earned praise for being more inclusive and respectful, the degree to which these surface changes have penetrated the culture of the school system seems modest.

A long-time parent leader recently remarked that "it is an enormous victory the [LSCs] have survived and still have power, because there has been so much effort to undermine that power." While not all Chicago reform participants so openly state this, it is not an uncommon sentiment. It can be difficult to find LSC members who do not feel like junior partners in school reform.

In an era of declining resources and shifting priorities, the new challenge for LSCs and their supporters is to demonstrate relevance. Ironically, it may be No Child Left Behind (NCLB) —the new bogeyman of American public education—that provides LSCs with a needed opportunity to reassert their leadership and value. While the particulars of this law are open to debate, NCLB has incontrovertibly focused public attention on the challenges that face our public schools. The current CPS administration may well discover that thousands of elected parent, teacher, community, and student leaders are valuable allies to cultivate in the uncertain months ahead. LSCs and their grassroots supporters must find a way to take the first step.

4

The Importance of Social Trust in Changing Schools

David T. Gordon

At a 2002 conference on accountability and assessment at Harvard's Kennedy School of Government, dozens of education policymakers and scholars gathered to consider the implications of the No Child Left Behind Act, which had been signed into law by President George W. Bush earlier that year. During hours of discussion about the value of standardized test data, "coercive" accountability, and stakes high and low, a pesky question kept surfacing about the wildcard in all of this: the people who actually go to school every day to work and learn. Can excellent work be coerced from principals, teachers, and students simply by withholding diplomas, slashing funds, and publishing embarrassing statistics in the newspaper?

As states and school districts work at structuring new accountability mechanisms and mandating changes in instruction, they will do well to remember that school people and their relationships to one another will make or break reform. How do teachers relate to each other? How do school professionals interact with parents and community? What are principal-teacher relations like? The answers to such questions are central to determining whether schools can improve.

That's one lesson learned from Chicago's decade of school reforms, according to a book by Anthony S. Bryk and Barbara Schneider. In *Trust in Schools: A Core Resource for Improvement* (Russell Sage, 2002), the University of Chicago researchers examine the role of social relationships in schools and their impact on student achievement. Their conclusion? That "a broad base of trust across a school community lubricates much of a school's day-to-day functioning and is a critical resource as local leaders embark on ambitious improvement plans."

To make their argument, Bryk and Schneider build on a body of literature about social trust, including the work of Robert Putnam (Harvard) and Francis Fukuyama (Johns Hopkins) on the foundations of effective democratic institutions and economies. Putnam has shown that when citizens trust each other less and become less engaged in society, a country loses an asset—social capital—that is essential to collective problem-solving. (A 1997 study by Harvard School of Public Health researchers even found evidence that breakdowns in social trust lead to health problems and shortened lives.)

Bryk and Schneider contend that schools with a high degree of "relational trust," as they call it, are far more likely to make the kinds of changes that help raise student achievement than those where relations are poor. Improvements in such areas as classroom instruction, curriculum, teacher preparation, and professional development have little chance of succeeding without improvements in a school's social climate.

Of course, the essential value of good relationships to improving schools is not a new theme. School leaders such as Theodore Sizer and Deborah Meier have written eloquently about the power of high-quality personal relationships in schools. However, Bryk and Schneider take the bold step of seeking empirical evidence that links trust and academic achievement. In doing so, they draw on ten years of work in Chicago schools during a period of sweeping reform, using quantitative and qualitative research, longitudinal case studies of elementary schools, and in-school observation and interviews.

DEFINING TRUST

What is relational trust? Bryk and Schneider readily admit it is "an engaging but also somewhat elusive idea" as a foundation for school improvement. But after thousands of hours spent observing schools—before, during, and after the school day—they suggest four vital signs for identifying and assessing trust in schools:

- *Respect.* Do we acknowledge one another's dignity and ideas? Do we interact in a courteous way? Do we genuinely talk and listen to each other? Respect is the fundamental ingredient of trust, Bryk and Schneider write.

- *Competence.* Do we believe in each other's ability and willingness to fulfill our responsibilities effectively? The authors point out that incompetence left unaddressed can corrode schoolwide trust at a devastating rate.
- *Personal regard.* Do we care about each other both professionally and personally? Are we willing to go beyond our formal roles and responsibilities if needed—to go the extra mile?
- *Integrity.* Can we trust each other to put the interests of children first, especially when tough decisions have to be made? Do we keep our word?

Trust is the "connective tissue" that holds improving schools together, write Bryk and Schneider. School administrators, teachers, parents, and students all have certain expectations of one another and their own obligations. Although power in schools, as in most institutions, is not distributed evenly—principals have more than teachers, teachers more than parents—all parties are ultimately dependent on each other to succeed, and therefore everyone is to some extent vulnerable.

Actions are important, but so are intentions. On a daily basis, trust is raised or diminished depending on whether the way we act—and why—is consistent with the expectations we have agreed to, the authors write. They contend that "the fulfillment of obligations entails not only 'doing the right thing,' but also doing it in a respectful way, and for what are perceived to be the right reasons."

In their research, Bryk and Schneider looked at trust through three lenses—the principal-teacher relationship, teacher-teacher trust, and ties between school professionals and parents, who represent both themselves and their children in this study. In doing so, the researchers identified a number of defining characteristics of such relationships.

PRINCIPALS AND TEACHERS

According to Bryk and Schneider, teachers seek a principal who communicates a strong vision for the school and clearly defines expectations. They also look for a principal who allocates resources and makes assignments in fair and consistent ways. Teachers want a principal to take an interest in both their professional and personal well-being. Does the principal encourage them to speak up without fear of retribution? Is the principal respected both as an educator and as an administrator? Does the school function smoothly? Does the principal put the interests of children ahead of personal and political interests?

Principals who are wishy-washy—who try to placate everyone—wind up losing everyone's trust. And those who don't deal with problem teachers in a firm but fair way are unlikely to keep a faculty's support. Incompetent teachers impede the progress of students and other teachers, who depend on their colleagues to be professional.

For their part, principals trust teachers who make efforts to improve their practice, demonstrate a willingness to try out new ideas and take risks, and show a "can-do" attitude. Trust is also better in schools where principals have hiring authority because it enables both the principal and the new teacher to decide whether the hire is a "good fit" for the school.

TRUST AMONG TEACHERS

Teachers' relationships with one another can often be more challenging than those between teachers and their bosses, the authors found. Teachers lean on each other in a number of ways in well-functioning schools. They have confidence that their colleagues in earlier grades have prepared students for subsequent work. Trust in colleagues' judgment, competence, and integrity helps teachers meet shared goals, standards, and expectations. Everyday activities such as planning instruction, setting discipline policies, and playground or lunchroom monitoring also depend on good will and mutual confidence.

Unfortunately, many schools are organized in ways that discourage trust building. Teachers are isolated from each other and have little time to discuss common or different views. This solo approach to teaching—the culture of "connoisseurship," as Harvard professor Richard F. Elmore puts it—sparks competition rather than collaboration.

Bryk and Schneider also identify procedural roadblocks in districts where teaching jobs get filled based on seniority and credentials rather than professionalism, or where incompetent teachers are protected by such rules.

TIES TO PARENTS

In general, research has demonstrated the importance of parents giving their support to schools. Such support can take many forms. Do parents help organize extracurricular events or raise funds? Do they support school disciplinary policies? Do they understand and help implement instructional strategies by making sure students do their homework and come to school prepared? Do they ensure that their kids get to school on time?

In Chicago, parental and community involvement in schools has been achieved partly through legislation. Under the 1988 reform act, each school has a local school council (LSC) composed of a principal, teachers, community leaders, and parents. Among the legally established duties of LSCs are to review and approve budgets, hire and fire principals, and oversee the development of "school improvement plans." So far, research by the Consortium on Chicago School Research has found that more than half of LSCs are highly effective governance organizations; about 30 percent perform well but need improvement; and 10 to 15 percent have significant problems, such as inactivity or sustained conflict with school leaders.

In most effective Chicago schools, good parent-school relations extend well beyond the formal duties of the LSC. Bryk and Schneider note that enlisting and cultivating parent support for schools may require bridging gaps in class, language, race, or ethnicity. Some ways of demonstrating regard for parents and families might be to create parent centers, offer programs for parents and students to take part in together, and invite parents to visit classrooms. For their part, parents need to demonstrate respect for teachers' professional judgment, particularly with regard to instruction and content, according to Bryk and Schneider. Input into what happens in the classroom is fine; involvement in a teacher's classroom work is not. Too often parents, especially those who are well educated, think they know better. Furthermore, those who regard themselves as school customers—as in "the customer is always right"—and not as partners in the education of their children can be especially disruptive. If schooling is to be a successful social enterprise, respect must go both ways.

WHAT THE EVIDENCE SAYS

The evidence from Chicago suggests that while not all schools with high levels of trust improve—that is, trust alone won't solve instructional or structural problems—schools with little or no relational trust have practically no chance of improving. Trust is a strong predictor of success.

Using data from the 1997 school year, Bryk and Schneider looked at levels of trust in schools in the top and bottom quartiles in terms of academic performance. In top-quartile schools, three-quarters of teachers reported strong or very strong relations with fellow teachers, and nearly all reported such relations with their principals. In addition, 57 percent had strong or very strong trust in parents. By contrast, at schools in the bottom quartile a majority of teachers reported having little or no trust in their colleagues, two-thirds said the same about their principals, and fewer than 40 percent reported positive, trusting relations with parents.

Of course, those statistics alone don't demonstrate a cause-and-effect link between trust and achievement, and the authors are careful not to make such a connection. After all, good relationships undoubtedly grow more easily in schools that are effective and are much harder to cultivate under failing conditions. But the authors do establish that schools with high levels of trust were far more likely to make improvements over time than those with low levels.

In a separate analysis, the researchers looked at 100 schools that made the greatest improvements on standardized tests in math and reading between 1991 and 1996 (before high-stakes measures were introduced in Chicago), and they examined 100 schools that made little or no improvement.

Matching those trends against teacher survey data, Bryk and Schneider found that schools with strong levels of trust at the outset of reforms had a 1 in 2 chance of making significant improvements in math and reading, while those with weak relationships had a 1 in 7 chance of making gains. And of the latter, the only schools that made any gains were those that strengthened trust over the course of several years; schools whose poor relationships did not improve had no chance of making academic improvements.

"These data provide our first evidence directly linking the development of relational trust in a school community and long-term improvements in academic productivity," the authors write. Even after controlling for factors such as high poverty rates, the statistical link between trust and school improvement is striking.

Certain organizational conditions make more fertile ground for trust to grow, according to Bryk and Schneider. Reducing student mobility aids efforts to build good relationships between school professionals and parents. Developing a sense of shared expectations and obligations is easier in schools where incompetent or uncooperative teachers can be removed. Voluntary association is also a factor. Administrators, teachers, parents, and students who get to choose their school are more likely to have a positive, trusting attitude about the school community.

Small schools—those with enrollments of 350 or fewer— also tend to have more trusting environments, Bryk and Schneider found. Those findings match the conclusions of other well-publicized studies, including one by the Bank Street College of Education in 2000, which found that teachers in small Chicago schools were more likely to have a strong sense of community and trust and be more open to change.

As we move into an era of national reform, the Chicago lesson is an important one. Good relationships and trust won't compensate for bad instruction, poorly trained teachers, or unworkable school structures, as Bryk and Schneider are careful to note. But by the same token, reform efforts are bound to fail if they ignore the importance of how teachers, principals, parents, and students interact—how the people behind the headlines work together. Like a shiny automobile with new parts and an empty gas tank, they're heading nowhere.

This article originally appeared in the Harvard Education Letter *(July/ August 2002).*

FOR FURTHER INFORMATION

A.S. Bryk and B. Schneider. *Trust in Schools: A Core Resource for Improvement.* New York: Russell Sage, 2002.

P. Wasley et al. *Small Schools, Great Strides.* New York: Bank Street College of Education, 2000.

5

How Trust Helped Transform a Small Chicago School

David T. Gordon

When Nancy Laho became principal of Burley Elementary School in the early 1990s, a number of obstacles hampered the small school in Chicago's Lakeview neighborhood. As in most failing urban schools, the curriculum lacked focus, teachers worked in isolation, and parents offered little support. Money for books, supplies, and building improvements was scarce. On standardized tests in math and reading, Burley's scores sagged at around the 25th percentile.

Laho's first act as principal demonstrated the kind of school she intended to run. She removed a large counter from the center of the main office to make herself more accessible to teachers and parents. Then she spread the word that no one needed an appointment to see her. "I wanted the office to be

47

wide open and welcoming, so people could walk in unimpeded," she says.

A decade later, Burley Elementary had become a bright spot in Chicago's partly sunny/partly cloudy reform. In 2002–2003, students performed in the 74th percentile in both reading and math in state rankings—this in a school where 85 percent of students are poor and where many of the 350 students speak English as a second language (about 65% are Hispanic).

With an academic plan focused on literacy and a flourishing bilingual program, teachers are working diligently at improving their practice, cultivating ties with parents, and supporting their principal. Much of the credit for that success is no doubt due to the sort of trust Laho inspired by removing the big office counter. That practical and hugely symbolic decision opened up lines of communication with staff and parents that enabled the school community to develop and agree on a direction in which to take the school.

Laho and her staff created a reading curriculum that requires all students to read independently in class each day and to hear teachers read aloud. Students must take books home, keep weekly reading journals, and have those journals signed by their parents to indicate that the work has been done. Parents attend monthly school assemblies where they read with their children and listen to students read favorite poems or passages from books. A local Starbucks provides free beverages for the event.

The Burley staff worked together to stop grade inflation and tighten standards by writing their own grade-by-grade frameworks. Special education teacher Nessy Moos, one of Laho's first hires back in 1993, says Laho has found just the right mix of being a strong leader without being autocratic. "We really have one view," she says. "There's no question Nancy is our leader, but she's also very supportive of us." The positive, trusting relationship between staff and principal has created good will among teachers, too. "Our relations are good, though sometimes controversial," says Moos. "Nancy hired people with strong personalities, people who are leaders. So we all have strong opinions about how things should be done. But there's no question everyone is committed. And we know ultimately that Nancy is our leader."

That confidence informs the professional development program that teachers themselves direct. Since they have helped develop the curriculum, each teacher knows what others in the building are teaching, and how. They present case studies, discuss books about teaching, and consider questions about learning and instruction. "We own the practice," says teacher Rusty Burnette.

Respect for Laho's leadership and integrity has helped the Burley staff weather a significant amount of turnover. By her second year, she had replaced six of the 15 teachers on staff, and she makes no apology for "encouraging" those who don't believe in the school's mission, especially its reading program, to work elsewhere. "When you counsel out staff, you have to do it in a way that shows respect," she says. "If you don't, teachers will rally and unite behind that person, even if they don't support their practice. Things like that can tear your staff to shreds if you're not careful."

PARENTS AND COMMUNITY

Knowing that any successful turnaround of a school requires the support and input of parents, the staff has worked hard to develop better ties to parents. Before Laho took over, Burley parents were fractured along racial, ethnic, and class lines, says Steve Renfro, a bilingual lead teacher with 13 years' experience at Burley. Today the school has an active, diverse Parent Teacher Association that provides much-needed support for academic and extracurricular efforts.

Laho sets the tone with her open, hardworking style. "The principal here is very accessible," says parent Tanya Suawicz. "She is easy to reach and responds quickly, so you know if there's a problem, it will get addressed. You know what she's going to do and why. She always tells us her reasons." PTA president Faith Spencer adds, "[Laho] doesn't always agree with parents but she always gives a fair hearing. We respect that."

Teachers get thumbs up, too. "You don't feel like you're bothering teachers when you visit a class," says Awilda Salzedo, treasurer of the PTA, who was impressed enough with Burley to transfer her children there from a parochial school. "They're welcoming."

The PTA shows its appreciation for teachers by making them dinner, giving them flowers, or giving them gift certificates to buy school supplies—money that would normally come out of a teacher's pocket. And this year it organized a volunteer group of "Homeroom Moms" to help teachers with time-consuming work, such as recruiting other parents to take part in school events. "So far it's worked really well," says Elsie Rosa, the PTA vice president. "We don't think teachers should have to get bogged down with all those details. They should focus on teaching kids." PTA members offer to serve as translators at school meetings in order to encourage Latino parents to take part.

For her part, 2nd-grade teacher Kary Eichstaedt invites parents "to hang out in class and check out the room," and she distributes a weekly newsletter informing them of upcoming curriculum units to encourage them to do "prelessons" at home. Meanwhile, Renfro and the school's Bilingual Advisory Council host workshops and classes on such topics as computer skills, alcohol and drug prevention, and "How to Talk to Your Maturing Teen."

"The challenge is to break down some cultural inhibitions about getting involved," says Renfro. "For example, some parents who have come from other countries are used to very authoritarian schools, schools where, if parents confronted the principal, the kids would pay. So some are reluctant to talk to [Principal Laho] if something's wrong. I end up hearing their concerns and relaying them to her anonymously."

The outreach is paying off. But as teacher Rusty Burnette points out, the true measure of a school's success will always come back to instruction. "The biggest influence on parent involvement comes from students themselves. If they're happy and they're learning, the parents have a reason to get excited," he says. Indeed, the enthusiasm and teamwork among teachers, parents, students, and administrators that pervade the old building on West Barry Avenue are every bit as remarkable as Burley's rising test scores.

This article originally appeared in the Harvard Education Letter *(July/ August 2002).*

A CONVERSATION WITH PRINCIPAL NANCY LAHO

In an interview with the Harvard Education Letter *published in 2002, Nancy Laho talked about what she learned in a decade at the helm of the Burley Elementary School. Later that year, Laho was promoted—first to the top position at one of the 24 new instructional areas that were created in 2002–2003, and then to the central office, where she is now in charge of improving the recruitment, retention, and training for Chicago's principals.*

On communicating with parents

I tell parents they can say whatever they need to. It doesn't have to be good news. I want them to be honest. Sometimes what they say and how they say it is upsetting, but I try hard not to let that show because the important thing is that they be heard. Sometimes that's all they want.

I'll admit I'm better at reacting to parent input than I am at seeking it out. I have a lot of conflict over this. I know intellectually that parent input is important. On the other hand, I base my decisions on a lot of experience, so I'm not always sure how much input I want. How will I use that information? How can I make it constructive?

For example, one issue on the table for two years now is the desire of a large group of parents to have foreign-language study in school. That would not be one of my priorities—I don't know how to fit it into the school day without losing something valuable—but I'm discussing it with parents because their voice is strong. And they're helping me think of ways to make it work, perhaps in an afterschool setting, even if it's for a fee. We haven't made a decision yet, but they know I take them seriously and that my goal is to figure out how to do it in a reasonable way.

On communicating with teachers

With staff it's the same thing: I hear them out and I share my thinking with them. For example, I know already that we are going to have to reorganize next year and make changes [in assignments]. I could just make those changes. That's my right as principal. I could put a notice in everyone's mailbox and that would be that. But what would that gain me? So I explain why I'm doing something even if it's not really up for discussion. I ask for their support and always try to give a little perk—maybe it's extra money in their budget for instructional materials or supplies, which is so valued by teachers—as a reward for cooperation.

Part of integrity is being predictable. People should have a basic idea how you will act or react. If they're in the guessing game, they can't trust you. You don't always have to agree but you have to communicate. If people are worried or grumbling, it will get back to you. There aren't many secrets in small schools. That has to be nipped in the bud. Get people together. Let them know we are all responsible for the climate we work in. That's a big part of community and trust building.

Solving problems is often a matter of clarifying perspective, of helping people see that they have to consider the needs of the whole school, that a particular program may need more resources at this time, and while that may not look fair or equal in the short range, it is ultimately right for the whole school. When I was a classroom teacher [for 17 years], I thought I had a schoolwide perspective. But when I became a principal, I realized that teachers very much live inside the four walls of their class. They have to advocate for their students, and there's something wrong if they don't. But principals have to advocate for all the students, for the whole school.

Good communication is not always enough to come to agreement, but hopefully there's enough respect so that teachers can live with a tough decision. Also important: as a principal I realize that sometimes I'm the one that has to be dissatisfied. Sometimes I have to realize that this is not the most important issue in the world and let someone have their way. Give and take is important. But it's a very natural and proper struggle. Fortunately, there's enough trust and collegiality here [at Burley] that we ride those waves well.

6

Parents as School Reformers

Madeline Talbott

As head organizer of the grassroots community organization Illinois ACORN (Association of Community Organizations for Reform Now), Madeline Talbott has been prominently involved in efforts to engage and empower parents in the school reform process in Chicago.

I n the fall of 2003, a news report about Chicago Public Schools (CPS) quoted school officials as saying that the problem of teacher quality had become less about recruitment and more about retention of teachers in hard-to-staff schools.

What wasn't said was that parents and community organizations, who have played an increasingly sophisticated role in improving education in Chicago's public schools, have led the way in emphasizing teacher quality, recruitment, and retention. Over the past 15 years, parents and communities have become increasingly involved in improving teaching and learning at both the classroom and the district level.

This is a far cry from the way things once were. Before Chicago school reform began in 1988, parents and community organizations were relegated at best to the roles of volunteers and fundraisers in the schools; at worst they were considered outsiders and interlopers. The voice of community organizations interested in education was largely limited to issues such as school closings, drug activity, crime, and unsafe playgrounds. They rarely had a say in the quality of teaching and learning in the classroom.

ACORN members can remember the days before reform, when parents had to pass through pretty severe screening systems just to enter a school. Once inside, they often felt less than welcome. There are countless stories of parents having to wait for hours to speak to a principal and never having phone calls returned. Sometimes they wondered if the principal really worked there at all.

"You had to have an appointment or a reason that was cleared by the administration to even walk into most school buildings," said Gwendolyn Stewart, mother of five grown children who went through the Chicago public schools during that time. "If you were not a regular at the school, you were immediately under suspicion the moment you walked in, guilty of something until proven innocent."

As for community organizations, they often had to get approval from the huge central bureaucracy located in three cavernous buildings on Pershing Road on Chicago's South Side to enter a school or move a program into a school. Being told to get approval from Pershing Road was the equivalent of being told that whatever you were proposing would never happen.

THE RISE OF LOCAL SCHOOL COUNCILS

With the passage of the first school reform law in 1988, things changed dramatically for parents and community organizations that were interested in educational improvement. With local school council (LSC) elections, all kinds of people started running for office and campaigning on a school-improvement platform. More than 80 members of ACORN ran for local school councils and won at 31 schools. These were low- and moderate-income parents and community residents; their campaigns included distributing flyers to parents outside of school as children were being picked up, going door to door in the neighborhood to discuss school issues and round up votes, and speaking at candidate assemblies at the schools.

Word spread through these campaigns that the LSCs could choose a new principal and control part of the budget at the school. Parents and community residents were catapulted from their positions as volunteer fundraisers and cafeteria monitors to elected office as members of the council that hired the principal and allocated funds. It was a heady time, and the principals changed their approach to voters and candidates almost immediately.

"Once it became clear to the principals that their job future was dependent on parents and community residents, schools started welcoming us all," says Imogene Somerville, who ran for local school council in 1989 and served many terms on the LSC at Henson Elementary. "Suddenly the principal was looking us in the eye when he talked to us, inviting us in to talk. We were no longer invisible or outsiders. He asked my opinion about things going on at the school, and shared his strategies and plans. Nothing like that had ever happened before," she continued.

DEEPENING INVOLVEMENT IN SCHOOLS: NEW CHALLENGES

At the same time, some parents started to get involved in teaching and learning. Newberry Math and Science Academy, located on the Near North Lakefront, set up a curriculum committee. One parent who attended the meeting said, "I don't even know what this is about. I know how to do bake sales for the schools. I'm used to helping the teacher on field trips. But what am I supposed to do with the curriculum?"

Eventually, some parents at some schools started to get it. They didn't have to be experts on curriculum, but they had to make sure that the faculty at their schools were talking to the experts and setting up the best educational program they could. Parents in effect needed to become sophisticated questioners and monitors of their children's education.

But it took a while for parents and community groups to make schools understand what real involvement looked like. And not every school saw immediate progress. For some schools the LSC experience was confusing, and years were spent trying to figure out the new governance system and to get LSC members trained and attending meetings.

Even when that happened, the LSCs in many schools started to replace the existing parent involvement mechanisms. Where parents made the mistake of thinking that the "LSC will handle it," parent involvement actually dropped after school reform. Eventually, school communities began to understand that the LSCs, with only six parents on each council, were not a replacement for organized parents.

THE VALLAS YEARS

There was another surge in parent and community involvement during the years when Paul Vallas served as CEO of the Chicago schools. Vallas understood money and politics, and his presence galvanized community organizations and parent groups to get active and involved. He came to be hated by many school reform advocacy organizations, but not necessarily by the community organizations and parent groups. Vallas could count. If he felt that you had no real community or parent base, he ignored you. But he cared about organizations with a base, and he was very clear that he would reward his friends and punish his enemies. If you worked with him he would deliver, at least at first.

Because Vallas moved a lot of money around and freed up significant funds for capital improvements, organized pressure on the school district could net a neighborhood a new school, or at least new windows. As a result, lots of groups got involved in education issues. Many of those issues were brick-and-mortar ones, rather than teaching and learning, but at least organized forces got closer to the schools and the classrooms as a focus for their activity.

During the Vallas years, some community organizations and parent groups were able to access Annenberg funding to help pay for much-needed technical assistance and leadership development expenses. But even when experts knew the ingredients of successful schools, they didn't always know how to get those ingredients into each school. It seemed to require a mix of very good school leadership, a committed faculty with a great professional development program, and lots of parent and community expectations and support, along with the financial and other resources to make this all possible.

Lots of community organizations and parent groups were able to build their own constituencies by inviting Vallas out to neighborhood or school meetings, where he would promise to deliver what the constituents wanted. For a number of years, his presence helped to increase the amount of parent and community participation in the schools because he was charismatic, the schools were improving, he had found money for school improvement through his reorganization of the bureaucracy and the good economy, and he liked to make promises.

TEACHER QUALITY AND DISTRICTWIDE EFFORTS

When money ran low and groups got tired of promises that were rarely kept, Vallas' stock fell. But by this time parent involvement was active and growing, and parents were looking for ways to influence what went on in the classroom.

In the meantime, the search for ways to improve teaching and learning came in the form of many different approaches to school improvement. Parent and community groups didn't want to become the educators, but they wanted to make sure that their children had the best possible educators and resources in their schools—changes that would require work at the district and state level, as well as in the community and school.

In Chicago, a good principal could be hired at the school level, but recruiting a highly qualified teaching force for low-income and low-performing schools couldn't be done effectively at that level. Parents at Mason Elementary at first tried running ads and recruiting their own teachers. Though it was a great learning experience and the principal was supportive of their efforts, it became clear that a much more sophisticated recruitment strategy was needed.

With that goal in mind, ACORN parents went to the Board of Education in early 2000 with a demand for quality teachers to fill the many teaching vacancies in their schools. With the aid of a newly reformed teacher recruitment process established by the Board, by the start of the next school year, September 2001, CPS had hired more teachers than ever before and the schools in ACORN neighborhoods were reporting a much smoother start to the school year. Now there was a teacher in every classroom, but there were still problems: Were they fully certified teachers with content knowledge in their grade level or subject area?

In 2002, ACORN found new handles in its quest for highly qualified teachers in low-income and low-performing schools in the form of No Child Left Behind (NCLB), which included a focus on teacher quality and an emphasis on parent involvement. Among other things, the law requires school districts to notify parents if their children are being taught for more than four weeks by a teacher not fully certified in subject-matter knowledge.

Parents marched on the Illinois State Board of Education in the summer of 2002 to demand that NCLB teacher-quality provisions be followed, and again in October that year to demand that parents receive the notice that the law required about the qualifications of their teachers. As a result, CPS took the law seriously and started sending notices out later that year. In turn, the notices helped build parent interest.

Nothing matters more to the promise of equal opportunity laid out in the American dream than the quality of education. The advent of school reform in Chicago created a climate that by and large encouraged parents and community organizations to feel that they could make a difference in the quality of public education. A number of community and parent groups then felt challenged to figure out a role for themselves in improving teaching and learning in the classroom. Many Chicago organizations are making progress and still fighting for adequate resources so that their children will have access to that dream. We have miles to go before we sleep, but active parents and community residents, combined with laws that give them leverage, like school reform and parts of NCLB, can result in real change and real improvements in our schools.

7

Moving Instruction
to Center Stage

David T. Gordon

"It's about instruction, stupid." That 2001 headline, which appeared in *Catalyst*, the magazine of record about Chicago school reform, says a lot about what has happened—and what hasn't—in the first decade of reforms. Despite some notable successes at individual schools, few would suggest that more than a decade of reform has produced the demonstrable gains in student achievement that was once expected. The question is why? One answer heard more often than not these days is "instruction."

Earlier in this book, I write about research showing the importance of strong, trusting relationships in schools—the power of social trust as an agent of school reform. In successful schools, the development of trust between administrators and teachers—and among teachers themselves—depends in large part on the amount of respect they have for each others' instructional abilities. Trust begins first and foremost with the question: Is this person committed to and capable of high-quality teaching?

The Consortium on Chicago School Research—a group of researchers from local universities, community groups, and the school system—has conducted a number of studies in an effort to identify why some Chicago schools are improving while most are not. Much of that work has focused on instruction. A survey of Consortium reports reveals some of the earmarks of improving schools.

1. Improving schools have a coherent instructional program.

This requires a common framework for learning—literacy is one possibility—that gives shape to curriculum, instruction, and assessment. It also requires that principals organize personnel and resources only in ways that support and advance those core goals. In short, the school day revolves around instruction.

Researchers measured the coherence of school programs based on these characteristics through a variety of data, including surveys of more than 1,000 teachers throughout the system and field studies from 11 high-poverty elementary schools with a variety of instructional approaches (see the report entitled "School Instructional Program Coherence: Benefits and Challenges"). From 1993 to 1997, schools with coherent instruction had a 12 percent increase in scores on the Iowa Test of Basic Skills; schools without a coherent plan showed no improvement and in some cases saw their scores drop.

Coherence shouldn't be confused with programming, the researchers note. Some schools try a number of initiatives—all of which may have merit and meet real student needs—and still are plagued by low student achievement. Why? In many cases because, as the report says, the principal and the teachers "find themselves faced with a large and fragmented array of school improvement grants, programs, and partnerships that rarely afford them the time or support to adopt and master practices that may improve student learning." In successful schools, focus takes precedence over flair.

The report also notes that coherence doesn't imply heavy-handed leadership or inflexibility. In fact, it is more likely to result from a mix of top-down and bottom-up strategies—strong leadership working in tandem with teachers who have a stake in the work of the whole school and some decision-making role. For instructional coherence to work, a school's teachers must be invested in making the strategy work.

2. Improving schools offer challenging instruction.

In studying the impact of the $54 million Chicago Annenberg Challenge, the Consortium has produced a series of reports examining the intellectual demands of classroom assignments. The researchers favor the framework of high-quality or "authentic intellectual work," which they define as involving the "construction of knowledge" through "the use of disciplined inquiry" that leads to "discourse, products, or performances that have value beyond school."

Using work samples and assignments from the 3rd, 6th, and 8th grades, the initial report ("The Quality of Intellectual Work in Chicago Schools: A Baseline Report"), published in

1998, showed that most Chicago students got assignments that emphasized rote learning, work that can be valuable for developing a base of knowledge but that does not necessarily give students the opportunity to develop and demonstrate interpretive abilities, organizational skills, a deeper understanding of concepts and how they connect, or other "higher thinking" skills—that is, the kind of intellectual work that may become essential as the so-called knowledge economy grows. The study found that when high-quality assignments were given—which was seldom—the quality of student work was also higher. The researchers note that this is not to say that students who receive low-quality assignments couldn't do better, but rather that the opportunity to show what they know is limited by the assignments.

A subsequent report ("Authentic Intellectual Work and Standardized Tests: Conflict or Coexistence?") found that students in the 3rd, 6th, and 8th grades who received such assignments scored higher on the Iowa Test of Basic Skills than those who didn't. For example, in classrooms with high-quality assignments, scores topped the national average by about 1.2 percent. In contrast, students in classes with low-quality assignments fell below the national average between 0.6 and 0.8 percent. Similar results were reported on the Illinois Goals Assessment Program (IGAP).

The high achievers include those living in the most disadvantaged socioeconomic conditions—a rebuttal, say the authors, to those who say that a back-to-basics approach is the best way to get students in such circumstances to achieve at higher levels. In fact, say the authors, embedding basic skills in challenging, "authentic" assignments can accomplish a number of instructional goals at once.

3. Improving schools keep pace in instruction.

Consortium research has shown that many Chicago schools do not offer grade-level instruction to their students (see the report "Setting the Pace: Opportunities to Learn in Chicago's Elementary Schools"). For example, researchers discovered that in different schools introductory lessons on the parallelogram were being taught in the 2nd, 5th, 8th, and 10th grades —essentially offering 2nd-grade lessons to students in all the classes.

In slow-paced classes on literature, students repeated the same kinds of exercises year after year. Students in both the 2nd and 10th grades were asked to identify a book's setting, events, and main characters. In contrast, in classrooms where study was paced to grade level, those same 2nd graders would be asked in the 5th grade to identify idioms and guess their meanings; in the 8th grade they might have to cite examples of hyperbole and explain its usefulness as a writing device; by the 10th grade, they would be expected to engage in detailed analysis of plot, including the uses of foreshadowing, flashback, and irony. In each of these classes, assignments built on prior learning.

A number of factors may slow the introduction of new material, according to the report. Teachers may rely too heavily on review and repetition, particularly in the weeks leading up to preparation for state-mandated achievement tests. The tests themselves and the stakes they carry may undermine teachers' belief that it is crucial to go beyond "teaching to the test." Weak homework assignments (or none at all), poor classroom management, and low expectations can also slow the pace.

4. Improving schools bolster instruction with social support.

While students in such schools are challenged to achieve at high levels, they also benefit from such supports as tutoring and good relationships with teachers. Social support and challenging instruction must go hand in hand, says the Consortium report "Social Support, Academic Press, and Student Achievement: A View from the Middle Grades in Chicago." The phrase "know every child" has become a familiar mantra in discussions of school improvement, and personal relationships have indeed proven to be a key part of better learning. But it's not enough. Those relationships must also be geared toward instructional improvement. "Teachers who are friendly toward their students but do not demand serious academic effort are not helping students reach their full potential," the researchers write. Likewise, assigning challenging work without giving students the necessary support will be counter-productive.

5. Improving schools emphasize "interactive" instruction.

In a high-stakes testing environment, should teachers use so-called didactic methods—that is, lectures, drill and practice, and worksheets that encourage students to memorize facts and procedures—or an "interactive" approach that emphasizes inquiry-based, hands-on activities, knowledge-building discussions, and projects that connect students to their larger world?

Of course, it's not an either/or question; nearly all teachers use a mix of styles. But the Consortium report "Instruction and Achievement in Chicago Elementary Schools" shows that, in a single school year, Chicago elementary school students in classes with high levels of interactive instruction scored higher on year-end tests than the city average—5.1 percent higher in math, 5.2 percent in reading. Students in mostly didactic classrooms scored below the city average in both—3.9 percent lower in math, 3.4 percent in reading. The researchers suggest that students who learn in interactive classrooms through the eight-year course of elementary school may end up a year ahead academically of those who receive didactic instruction.

Whether teachers use didactic or interactive means, all of them face the issue of how—and how much—to review previous lessons before moving forward in the curriculum. The Consortium study found that students scored better on year-end tests when instructional review was limited—4.2 percent better than the city average in math, and 4.1 percent better in reading. "Although reviewing familiar content may help build a solid knowledge base for new learning, this could also diminish learning by taking away from teaching new material," the authors write.

Didactic instruction and review get used most after 5th grade; where behavioral problems and irregular attendance are usual; where students are low achievers; in large schools; and in schools with a predominantely African American and/or low-income student body—all of which may suggest that those who might benefit most from interactive instruction aren't getting it, according to the report.

6. Improving schools use effective professional development to upgrade instruction.

To teach their children well, schools must teach their teachers well. It is what ties together these other characteristics of improving schools. Instructional focus, appropriate pacing, effective teaching practice, challenging assignments, and supportive relationships are greatly enhanced by high-quality professional development, according to the Consortium report "Teacher Professional Development in Chicago: Supporting Effective Practice."

What is effective professional development? According to a growing consensus among education professionals cited by the Consortium reports, such development gets teachers to reflect in an organized way on their practice, assess student work together, share resources and strategies, and build a sense of collective responsibility for improvement of the whole school. Such development emphasizes ongoing learning in terms of both subject matter and teaching practices. It is frequent, intensive, and includes follow-up exercises; centers around a school's instructional goals; and includes perspectives from beyond the school's walls—work with outside coaches, perhaps, or with education researchers—that can freshen the pool of ideas.

To achieve this requires certain organizational supports: strong instructional leadership from principals, sufficient time, and a school culture that encourages innovation and open discussion about what's working and what's not.

Much of the Consortium's research suggests that professional development will make or break reform. For example, the study on pacing cited above demonstrated that teachers were more likely to teach at grade level in schools with strong professional communities where they had had common goals and frequent communication about instruction. Similar findings were reported in the study on interactive and didactic instruction.

A NEW ERA IN CHICAGO?

Of course, these are not the only factors leading to improved schools, nor are they the only ones Chicago reformers have tried. Chicago's first decade of reform focused largely on issues of school organization and governance. In the first phase of reform from 1990 to 1995, decentralization was the focus. Each school was given control of its curriculum and budget through an elected local school council made up of the principal, teachers, parents, and community leaders. In phase two, beginning in 1995, the central administration under Mayor Richard M. Daley and the chief executive officer of schools, Paul Vallas, imposed some necessary fiscal and administrative discipline on the system and oversaw the introduction of a high-stakes accountability system centered around standardized tests. Test scores rose and reached a plateau in 1999. Yet the city still had no systematic, coherent instructional strategy.

That may be changing in phase three under schools CEO Arne Duncan, who took over in 2001. Duncan's first major effort was to improve reading in K–8 schools. Schools are now required to set aside two hours of instructional time each day to teach reading, divvying that time up into the framework's four areas: word knowledge, comprehension, writing, and fluency. They are also mandated to use strategies supported by research. A high school version of this program has also been implemented. In the meantime, reading specialists have been assigned to a large and growing number of schools, starting with the city's bottom 25 percent in reading. All schools have received money to create classroom libraries and funds for teacher and principal training in promoting literacy. After years of wrangling over governance and organization, is classroom instruction finally moving front and center in Chicago's reform efforts?

This article originally appeared in the Harvard Education Letter (September/October 2002).

FOR FURTHER INFORMATION

The reports cited are all published by the Consortium on Chicago School Research, 1313 E. 60th St., Chicago, IL 60637; 773-702-3364; fax: 773-702-2010. www.consortium-chicago.org

They can be obtained by contacting the Consortium or downloaded at no charge from the website (Adobe Acrobat format).

A.S. Bryk, J.K. Nagaoka, and F.M. Newmann. "Chicago Classroom Demands for Authentic Intellectual Work: Trends from 1997–1999." 2000.

V.E. Lee, J.B. Smith, T.E. Perry, and M.A. Smylie. "Social Support, Academic Press, and Student Achievement: A View from the Middle Grades in Chicago." 1999.

F.M. Newmann, A.S. Bryk, J.K. Nagaoka. "Authentic Intellectual Work and Standardized Tests: Conflict or Coexistence?" 2001.

F.M. Newmann, G. Lopez, and A.S. Bryk. "The Quality of Intellectual Work in Chicago Schools: A Baseline Report." 1998.

F.M. Newmann, B. Smith, E. Allensworth, and A.S. Bryk. "School Instructional Program Coherence: Benefits and Challenges." 2001.

J.B. Smith, V.E. Lee, and F.M. Newmann. "Instruction and Achievement in Chicago Elementary Schools." 2001.

J.B. Smith, B. Smith, and A.S. Bryk. "Setting the Pace: Opportunities to Learn in Chicago's Elementary Schools." 2001.

M.A. Smylie, E. Allensworth, R.C. Greenberg, R. Harris, and S. Luppescu. "Teacher Professional Development in Chicago: Supporting Effective Practice." 2001.

8

School Improvement at Benito Juarez High School

Richard G. Gelb

As curriculum coordinator at Benito Juarez Community Academy, Richard G. Gelb has been at the center of a series of internal and external school improvement efforts focused on literacy instruction for the school's students, many of whom come from bilingual programs. His school-level experience of the Chicago Public Schools' external partner program is eye-opening.

Benito Juarez Community Academy is located in the Pilsen neighborhood on Chicago's Lower West Side, a gateway for immigrants since before the time of the Great Chicago Fire. The school itself was built in 1977 through the political efforts of community organizations. Since its inception, Juarez has served predominantly Hispanic students, over 90 percent of whom are of Mexican heritage. Of approximately 1,700 students, more than 90 percent come from low-income households, and, more important, 80 percent were at one time or are currently in a bilingual program.

Incoming freshmen at Juarez are on average two years behind in reading. In essence, the school's task is to increase students' literacy abilities by three years in the space of one—a feat that schools that maintain selective enrollments or whose students are from predominantly native English-speaking backgrounds can hardly imagine. Nor would they ever need to be concerned with being on "probation" or in being "restructured."

As in many other school districts, the Chicago Public Schools (CPS) revamped its bilingual education policy in 2000 to mandate that students could only remain in a bilingual program for a maximum of three years. This directive had dramatic implications for schools such as Juarez. For eight years prior to the mandate, 27 percent of the school's population had been in a bilingual program. Since the mandate has been implemented, that number has been reduced to 15 percent, dramatically increasing the number of limited-English students who are being asked to compete academically in all subject areas with English-speaking students.

CURRICULUM COORDINATOR

Increasing student achievement is the primary objective of every school administrator, and many consultants have earned their living promoting ways to accomplish this task. What has been less conspicuous in the pedagogical chatter surrounding school improvement is the concept that schools, like all organizations, are political arenas where power relationships swirl around issues of overtime pay, staff positions, and status.

Over the past 15 years, my role at Juarez has evolved, often due to the changing demands of central office administrators or to the revolving door of principals at the school. I began teaching English at Juarez in 1987, and since that time I have worked for six principals, five of them in the last nine years. In 1999, I was asked by my principal to serve as the school's curriculum coordinator, acting as a liaison between the administration and the faculty. The previous principal had been removed by the Board of Education over a grade-change scandal, and the previous curriculum coordinator had alienated many teachers.

Essentially, my job is to raise students' scores on standardized tests, which have included during my tenure the following alphabet soup of assessment acronyms: TAP, CASE, EXPLORE, PLAN, PSAE, and ACT. That is the goal. The vehicle that CPS has designated to help schools like Juarez improve is staff development, with the help of an "external partner."

External Partner 1: Department of Accountability, 1999–2000

My first order of business was to gain consensus as to the course of action we needed to take. I first formed an Interdisciplinary Literacy Team, with each department providing a representative. This team met with consultants from the Department of Accountability (DA), the first of our school's many external partners during the past four years.

The DA was a part of the same CPS office that determined whether a school would need to undergo restructuring, which could include the drastic action of replacing a school's staff and administration. Working with the DA made good political sense in that they would know how to raise test scores, and they did provide my team with a new direction and focus. Unfortunately, they exhibited the same dictatorial traits as the former curriculum coordinator I had replaced.

Their initial move was to institutionalize vocabulary instruction in the form of the "Word of the Day." Administrative lore says that if you are exposed to something seven times, it will be learned. I have found that once such a notion is presented to the CPS bureaucracy, it soon becomes an undisputed "fact." Following this theory, students were to learn the same vocabulary word in each class, every day. Students thus would be exposed to a new word each day throughout the school year. The words were discipline-specific, with each month's list highlighting a different department. Can you imagine presenting a set of decontextualized math words in your English class or vice versa every day?

We did as we were told, however, and inflicted this theory on our students. As the DA suggested, we also adopted timed reading in all of the core subjects—a practice that was only marginally contextualized and was extremely boring for the students and teachers. We selected a new reading comprehension strategy each month and introduced the Cornell note-taking system. Although test scores rose, the gruff, disorganized administrative style of the external partner alienated the principal and teachers. They achieved their objective, which was to help us raise standardized test scores, but scores on other assessments did not improve. Their contract was not renewed.

External Partner 2: University of Illinois at Chicago (UIC), 2000–2001

The next year, we changed external partners. The Department of Accountability had provided us with some effective strategies, but our internal team noted areas that still needed improvement.

The new team from UIC was comprised of graduate students. They were very disorganized and did not have a long-range plan outside of improving TAP scores. Each month they focused on a different reading comprehension strategy. During the school year, we switched from the Word of the Day to Latin and Greek roots. We made the Cornell system optional. Teachers who preferred sustained silent reading (SSR) were allowed to use that instead of timed reading.

One additional objective, proposed by UIC professor Steve Tozer, was to build the capacity of the department chairs, who were designated members of the Literacy Team. Their input broadened the scope of the team to include improving CASE scores—subject area tests that were not part of the district's accountability system but were useful in helping the team make pedagogical adjustments. Schools such as Juarez actually benefited from the CASE, for it demonstrated that in some areas our teaching compared favorably with schools that maintained selective enrollments.

Still, in terms of literacy instruction the UIC team lacked organization and vision. I turned to Professor Tozer to help me develop my own literacy initiative, and he agreed to collaborate with me.

External Partner 3: UIC and the Chicago Area Writing Project, 2001–2002

The plan for this year called for a member from each department to become part of the Literacy Leadership Team. The Word of the Day was once again transformed—I chose the words from an ACT-preparation list. Despite a dramatic dip in our TAP scores, on the advice of the team we diminished the use of timed readings once again. The use of SSR was overwhelmingly the staff's fluency strategy of choice.

We also adopted some new approaches. Teachers from the Chicago Area Writing Project (CAWP) modeled reading comprehension strategies at our monthly three-hour, afterschool Literacy Team meetings. Teachers were paid a stipend to attend these meetings by our external partner. Following the presentation, teachers developed discipline-specific assignments using the strategies that were modeled. At the following department meeting, each member of the team made a presentation of the reading strategy to her/his department. Department members were then provided time to discuss and practice using the strategy. The strategy was then implemented throughout the school, and TAP scores for Juarez skyrocketed upward.

External Partner 4: UIC and the Chicago Reading Initiative, 2002–2003

Just as things seemed to be going well for Juarez, CPS again changed course, eliminating two of the main high school tests and implementing a new reading initiative program through-out the district. Professor Tozer and UIC continued to support the Literacy Team concept developed the previous year. Under the reading initiative, the Word of the Day evolved into the "literacy bellringer of the day" in each classroom. We contin-ued to use SSR, despite the fact that the reading initiative peo-ple did not advocate it.

IMPLICATIONS

The experience of the last few years has convinced me of a few key things. First, that school improvement efforts must not be solely focused on improving literacy in isolation. The core be-lief of the current literacy initiative being implemented by CPS is the conviction that one's ability to read impacts the success he/she can expect to achieve in school. Research data, however, has not been provided to support this claim, and it has been my experience that many school dropouts have high levels of literacy, while many students who graduate and even make the honor roll have low levels of literacy, compensated for by high levels of motivation. Literacy is important, but schools must also address issues of student motivation. Stu-dent literacy skills are a result of social conditions both inside and outside of school.

Second, consistency must be maintained. Each new ad-ministration brings a new set of expectations, as well as an ar-ray of political baggage. Without a stable administration and a stable set of test measures to determine our improvement, schools like Juarez will continue to be tossed from one initia-tive to another, like a derelict ship lost at sea.

Finally, all tests are unique, and therefore require special preparation. According to the staff at CPS, good teaching automatically equates with higher test scores. This is the equivalent of telling an NFL team to prepare for the Super Bowl as you would for any game. Today's tests require strategic preparation. Since it is the teachers who will prepare students to take the standardized tests, they should have the political control to make the decisions that impact the literacy instruction in their classrooms.

PART II

Policy and Politics

9

Establishing Accountability for Chicago Schools

Philip J. Hansen

Long-time principal Philip J. Hansen served from 1995 to 2002 as a key member of the Vallas education team, overseeing many parts of the accountability and "external partner" programs that were among the main—and most controversial—elements of the effort to improve school performance, especially among chronically low-performing schools.

As a Chicago Public School (CPS) principal, I had pretty much decided by 1995 that the CPS system was as bad as it could get. Despite all efforts at improvement, teacher strikes were rampant, test scores were declining, financially the system was going into bankruptcy, morale was low, and good students were leaving the system to go to parochial or suburban schools.

Then, in a late-summer meeting with newly appointed Board chairman Gery Chico and a small group of neighboring principals, we decided to pretty much go for broke, speak plainly, and let the chips fall where they may. Here was yet another new team and, generally speaking, we were skeptical and feeling somewhat beaten down by a system that did not seem to care about kids. We explained that our parents were demanding additional funding, systemwide financial stability, help with the physical conditions of our building, and, most importantly, strong leadership.

A few days later, I got a call from the new chief executive officer, Paul Vallas, and he asked me if I would leave my school and become the director of school intervention in the newly formed Office of Accountability. My initial question to him was, "Are you sure you have the right Phil Hansen?" However, after much serious thought and good advice from my family to say no, I accepted the position. In 1997, I became the chief accountability officer, a position I held until 2002.

Why? I did it because the new team seemed to share the same philosophical beliefs that I pounded home at the meeting with Gery Chico. People often look to this period from 1995 to 2001 and fail to grasp that there was, in fact, a strong philosophical foundation on which the Office of Accountability was established. It mirrored my beliefs as a principal, and so the opportunity to make these beliefs become policy was simply too good to pass up.

In those early years, starting in 1995, we knew that we had to be change agents for the system. In order to have any kind of impact, bold decisions had to be made. New plans had to be attempted. New options needed to be explored. We were encouraged to think in new and different ways. The system was totally broken, and we believed it was better to try and risk failure than to keep the status quo. The change had to be based on the belief in a strong accountability system and a strong belief that all children can learn.

Our initial visits to schools found some common themes that we immediately knew had to be addressed.

The most obvious was the lack of high standards and expectations from educators. Hard-working teachers and administrators would say the same thing over and over: "Give us better students and we will do a better job. We are doing the best we can with what we have." Clearly, the system could never move forward when the prevailing conversation in schools was how the instruction could be made easier for these students who were low performing. The mindset had to be changed.

Second, in too many schools it did not matter if the instruction or the leadership was poor. No one was watching to ensure accountability. As a principal, I had been so accountable that it became overwhelming. Parents would come to see me any time they perceived that there was a problem in their child's classroom. Neighbors would call me at school and at home if they thought the children were misbehaving on the way to or from school, or if the building looked like it needed some upkeep or repair. Community newspapers would publish our test scores and anything else that was going on in the school. My local school council was an intelligent, focused, and knowledgeable group who had high expectations for me and for the school. Most Chicago public schools did not have this kind of accountability. It became apparent that, as it often did not exist, there had to be a systemwide mechanism put in place to bring this level of accountability to schools.

Finally, there was the issue of bureaucratic inertia. Historically, a change in superintendent meant little more than a change in the stationery letterhead. In order to make the necessary changes, we all knew that the new administration had to have an impact. We had to make sure that people understood that we were symbolic of change, and that we weren't going to go away anytime soon.

And so we took action.

First, the new administration targeted the lowest performing schools in the city as the target group for change. During the 1995–1996 school year, these were the schools that had performed poorly on the Illinois Goals Assessment Program (IGAP) tests. The following year, the system moved away from the IGAP as the state was moving to a new test, and began to concentrate on the Iowa Tests of Basic Skills.

This measure of improvement was set in 1988 at the percentage of students at or above national norms, based on a 1988 norming. In order to show growth over a consistent measure, CPS continued to use the same one.

Our second goal was to provide strong support for schools that were struggling to meet these new accountability standards. There was no systemwide credibility for the central office, however, so we knew that we needed to bring in outside organizations—called "external partners"—to improve schools.

Toward that end, local colleges, universities, and nationally recognized educational organizations were utilized to assist schools in improving. Retired and successful principals were brought in to offer leadership and guidance in the probation process. Surely successful principals and universities would be able to move these schools forward, we thought. Business managers were put into these probation schools to free up the principals to become the instructional leaders that we rarely saw. And to complete the process, low-performing schools were visited by accountability teams and, in plain and straightforward language, we told schools what they were doing well, where they needed some help, and specifically how they could begin to improve.

Schools did begin to improve. Scores went up, people began to believe that this administration was different, and we began to see success stories in low-performing schools as many moved off probation. We also saw some schools that did not make progress and, as early as 1997, we set upon an aggressive plan to bring change to these schools. This was done through the removal of 11 principals in June 1997 and the reconstitution of five high schools at the same time. Critical to accountability was the urgent need for change, swift action, and consequences.

Principal removals were painful processes. It was necessary to hold a public hearing in each instance and to bring evidence to the hearing officer that a removal was justified. The Board then had to review the recommendation and make a final decision. But the difficulty was offset by the fact that these schools usually improved in both climate and in academics after this process.

Some people suggest that this process was mean-spirited. To these critics, I can only respond that, on many of our school visits, the teams actually left in tears at what they saw. We believed, and I still believe, that urban systems have waited too long for change. Each year that change does not take place, literally thousands of children lose the chance to become productive members of society. The urgency was absolutely necessary and much past due. And still is.

Some people suggest that we should have used another test or different measures of school improvement. In retrospect, it would have been good to take a more comprehensive and detailed picture of school improvement, though when we began to look at yearly growth and decline in the lowest quartiles, we did get a better and more comprehensive picture of student improvement.

But early attempts to change our measure were met with great skepticism from the press, which felt that we were doing what urban systems often do: bring in a new test with a new administration, declare improvement, and move on. We decided that we needed a measure that was consistent over time and could show past, present, and future progress. We also needed a measure that the larger community could understand. Parents, businesses, newspapers, politicians all could grasp "at or above national norms."

Perhaps most important, the external partner program continued to evolve as we learned valuable lessons about what worked and what didn't. For example, we soon discovered that colleges and universities were also struggling with how to turn around low-performing schools. To help with this, we instituted regular meetings with all external partners, encouraging them to share their victories and their concerns.

Similarly, we found that outside experts from across the nation often did not understand the Chicago schools, and the costs of hiring them were exorbitant, with half of the cost going toward flying them into Chicago and paying for their meals and lodging. We quickly decided to stick with locals.

At the same time, we also discovered that, while our probation managers were our best former and current principals, in some cases these principals were successful because of their personalities and their leadership skills. Neither of these could be transferred to principals on probation.

And last but not least, we found that freeing up principals to be instructional leaders by giving them business managers seemed like an excellent idea, but wasn't always what was needed most. In some cases, we discovered that principals were not really trained to be instructional leaders and were, in fact, more comfortable dealing with operational issues. So we developed new partnerships with the Chicago Principal and Administrators Association to offer more training and professional development for our school principals.

Reports often are critical of the probation process, but probation schools did show improvement during these years. We raised the probation bar more than once as the schools improved. Most schools that stayed on probation did so because we kept raising the bar. And many schools, even with the higher standards, were removed from probation. None of these schools was fond of the probation label, but they used it to bring urgency and focus to their instructional programs. These schools' principals and others used the probation process to bring urgency to the need for change. And these are just some of the schools that others can use as models to show that all schools can do a better job.

When people ask me if probation "worked," I usually tell them that we put 109 schools on probation in 1996, and that if we still were using the same criterion for probation today, we would have 13 schools on probation; only two of these are elementary schools. Schools at all performance levels improved. Today's low-performing schools are at a much higher level than they were in 1995. Yes, probation worked.

Equally important, the probation system continued to improve. As time passed, the system began to look at not only the "at or above" percentage, but also the percentage of students in the lowest quartile. Accountability also broadened to include all the people involved in improving education—principals, teachers, students, and even parents.

School improvement is not easy. Systemwide change is even more difficult, a constantly changing process. It remains a monumental challenge. But each year our schools have improved. The Vallas administration redefined the term *low performing*. This in itself is quite an accomplishment. The process has continued under the current administration. The urgency also continues.

10

Transition Programs for Retained Students: Segregation or Salvation?

Michael Sadowski

Beyond the metal detector, it looks like hundreds of other schools you might find across the United States —a place where teachers, administrators, and staff have worked hard to create a welcoming learning environment. Brightly painted walls, cheerful bulletin boards that announce school events and programs, and room signs made lovingly by hand belie the building's environs in Back of the Yards, a tough neighborhood on Chicago's South Side. The Samuel D. Proctor Academic Preparatory Center is in many ways a study in contrasts.

"In any large metropolitan environment like Chicago, there's so much going on every morning, every afternoon.

First we've got to make sure the students get here," says Doris Brown, an administrative staff member in charge of student discipline and support. "Once we get them here, we give them their hug and send them off to class."

Morning hugs for students who are having a rough day are part of the culture at Proctor, but so are smaller classes, more individualized attention, and more counseling and support personnel per pupil than Chicago's regular public high schools. The reason for this disparity is the special population that Proctor serves: students who have not met the criteria for graduation to high school.

Proctor is one of seven Academic Preparatory Centers (APCs) operated by the Chicago Public Schools (CPS) for this subset of students. Four of the APCs are in stand-alone buildings and three are housed within regular city high schools. The average APC serves somewhere between 150 and 200 students for one year, according to APC coordinator Elizabeth Ester.

Janell Taylor, director of the John H. Sengstacke APC, located south of the city's downtown Loop, says that her school also provides a nurturing environment that her academically needy students would not receive in a mainstream secondary school. "Kids get a whole lot more here than they may get elsewhere," says Taylor. "Once they leave and go on to some of these larger high schools, they're pretty much just a number."

A ROCKY HISTORY

Despite the strong sense of commitment that is apparent in the words of educators like Brown and Taylor, APCs have had a rocky and controversial history. Education advocacy groups in Chicago have criticized the APCs from the beginning as part of the city's controversial retention policy, which has dominated the local school reform debate over the past decade. Under the original form of the policy (which has been modified in recent years to include multiple criteria), 3rd, 6th, and 8th graders who did not achieve a certain score on the Iowa Test of Basic Skills (ITBS) were retained in grade if they could not raise their scores sufficiently by the end of a required summer school course (and if they did not receive a waiver). However, since another district policy bars students from attending elementary schools if they are or will turn 15 by December 1 of the academic year, Chicago needed to come up with a solution for its older students who couldn't be promoted under the first policy and couldn't be retained under the second. As a result, in 1997 city officials opened the first "transition centers," which were later renamed APCs.

Local advocacy groups accused the new centers of offering a watered-down curriculum designed almost exclusively to boost test scores. "The curriculum consisted of the morning reading drill and the afternoon math drill, and that was the program," says Julie Woestehoff, executive director of Parents United for Responsible Education (PURE), a local advocacy group representing parents of CPS students. "It was like extended summer school."

Scrutiny of the entire retention and promotion program reached a peak when PURE filed a complaint with the U.S. Department of Education's Office for Civil Rights (OCR) in 1999. The organization charged that the district's use of the ITBS as a single measure had a disproportionately negative effect on African American, Latino, and male students. PURE won its case against the district, and since 1999 Chicago has followed a modified version of its original retention and promotion policy, including the ITBS as one of several measures used to make such decisions.

Bolstered by its victory, PURE next targeted the APCs directly. The group filed another civil rights complaint with the OCR in 2001, this time charging the city with discrimination "in the establishment, intent, and operation" of the preparatory centers. "PURE believes that the APCs are educationally segregated and provide a substandard curriculum and program," PURE stated in its second complaint to the federal agency. In addition, PURE officials noted that the student bodies of the APCs were nearly 98 percent African American and Latino, compared with 85 percent across the city. PURE alleged that this disparity had led to higher dropout rates among this population.

In this second case, however, the OCR did not find evidence to support most of PURE's charges, including that APC students were subject to a test-driven, substandard program that lacked rigor and sufficient curricular and extracurricular opportunities. Instead, the investigation—based on a review of school district documents, visits to three APCs, and interviews with APC students, teachers, and administrators—found that both students and educators in APCs were more satisfied with their schools than many of their counterparts elsewhere in the city. Both groups cited smaller classes and more opportunities for individualized attention among the reasons why they believed the APC model works in their schools.

"I've worked in high schools for all of my career and I'm seeing, if anything, more challenges [being offered to APC students]," Proctor's Brown says.

The encouraging findings of the OCR investigation begged a question that seemed inconceivable just a few years before: Were the APCs actually providing a better education than high schools in the Chicago system? Woestehoff herself concedes that the APCs of today are a big improvement over the transition centers of the 1990s: "The APCs have changed a lot. I think partly because of our complaints and partly because of other people's criticisms, they have more services. They have added high school programs and high school credit, and they've got a fairly significant investment in counseling and other social services." Also, since the district now uses multiple measures to make retention and promotion decisions, APC teachers are freer to focus less on test prep and more on high school readiness.

LARGER QUESTIONS

In a time of increased attention to accountability, educators may feel especially compelled to provide remedial instruction to students whom they expect to perform poorly on high-stakes tests. As a result, transition programs like the APCs are cropping up in school systems around the U.S. But as researchers and advocates have noted, several questions remain unresolved about these sorts of pullout programs.

The first has to do with the stigma associated with requiring struggling students to attend school under separate circumstances, even if those circumstances are in some ways equal to or better than the "mainstream" alternative. The directors of both the Proctor and Sengstacke schools acknowledge that, at first, many students see their assignment to an APC as a defeat. "Most of the students who come to us are disappointed, as anyone would be if they haven't been able to go on and matriculate [in high school] as their peers did," says Proctor director Loretta Young-Wright. "Some of them are a little angry about it, some of them are sad and hurt, and we try to provide all kinds of supportive services to meet their needs." Both directors also say, however, that once enrolled in the APCs, most students appreciate the extra attention they receive and miss that attention once they move on to the relative anonymity of a large high school.

A second, related question has to do with possible connections between transition programs and dropping out. Here, the findings from Chicago are mixed. While the OCR investigation found that dropout rates among APC students were slightly lower than those for 9th graders in the city's high schools (10.8% vs. 12.2%), statistics from the Consortium on Chicago School Research, a group based at the University of Chicago, found that APC students were more likely than their peers to drop out in later high school years. Of course, there is no way to determine how many of these students would have dropped out had they not attended APCs. In addition, it is impossible to calculate the number of students who drop out before they even begin a transition program because they are discouraged by the prospect of not being able to attend high school. The Chicago Consortium found in a recent study that the number of 8th graders who have dropped out of the Chicago school system has risen by 38 percent since 1996, the year before the first APCs were opened.

A third concern about transition programs involves the racial segregation that often results from them. While many students and faculty in Chicago's APCs seem to believe that the benefits of the individualized attention outweigh the costs of being in a program that segregates youth racially and/or academically, this may not be the case everywhere. And, there may be other factors that complicate this issue in particular settings. In Chicago, many APC students travel on public transportation well beyond their neighborhoods to get to school, often, as Woestehoff puts it, through "hostile gang territory."

Fourth, the question of what happens to students after they leave the somewhat protected environment of an APC-like program concerns some researchers. A 2002 report by the Chicago Consortium found that students who go from APCs to high school have "difficulty getting and staying on track." The researchers note that students from APCs tend to take full course loads once they arrive in high school, but have trouble passing classes and earning enough credits to stay on the same academic level as their peers.

A MODEL PROGRAM?

Perhaps the most important question about Chicago's APCs has to do not with what happens to students for the short amount of time they are there, but whether the benefits they seem to get from smaller classes and extra support could be multiplied if similar programs could reach more students for longer periods of time.

"It would be wonderful if some of these schools could evolve into four-year high schools, or even two-year schools," Sengstacke director Taylor says.

Woestehoff agrees, but she suggests that such extra support would ideally be offered in mainstream high schools where lower-performing students could receive the help they need while still participating along with other students in a "normal" high school experience. This approach is in line with the way some researchers have resolved the retention-versus-social-promotion dilemma. They recommend promoting students so that they do not fall behind their age cohorts and become vulnerable to dropping out, but providing them with the support they need to succeed. "It may be that neither social promotion nor grade retention alone adequately serves the needs of youths who are doing poorly in school," writes Melissa Roderick, a University of Chicago researcher. "Research on grade retention has found that promotion with remediation provides more short-term academic benefits to youths than either retention alone, retention with remediation, or promotion alone."

Providing the level of remediation, individualized attention, and counseling available in APCs to all the at-risk students in the Chicago Public Schools—or in any large school system—would obviously be a tall order, given the paucity of financial resources currently available to public education. But this may be the only alternative to social promotion that does not segregate students, stigmatize them, or leave a substantial number of them behind as failures and dropouts before they even reach high school.

"[If students are struggling] you simply need to stop somewhere and help those kids," says Proctor's Young-Wright. "You could call it anything you want. You don't have to call it transition, you don't have to call it academic prep, you don't have to call it special ed. Just give the kids what they need."

This article originally appeared in the Harvard Education Letter *(March/April 2003).*

Editor's note: After this article appeared, CPS began relocating the transition centers to sites located in neighborhood high schools.

FOR FURTHER INFORMATION

A.B. Cholo. "Dropping Out in Grade School: Tough Promotion Policy Linked to Earlier Quitting." *Chicago Tribune*, August 11, 2002: C1–2.

C. Gewertz. "More Chicago Pupils Flunk Grade." *Education Week*, October 9, 2002.

S.R. Miller, E.M. Allensworth, and J.R. Kochanek. *Student Performance: Course Taking, Test Scores, and Outcomes (The State of Chicago Public High Schools: 1993 to 2000).* Chicago: Consortium on Chicago School Research, 2002.

D.R. Moore. *New Data about Chicago's Grade Retention Program Provides Further Proof That Neither Retention nor Social Promotion Works.* Chicago: Designs for Change, 2000.

M. Roderick, J. Nagaoka, J. Bacon, and J.Q. Easton. *Update—Ending Social Promotion: Passing, Retention, and Achievement Trends Among Promoted and Retained Students, 1995–1999.* Chicago: Consortium on Chicago School Research, 2000.

J. Temkin. "Transition Students: Most Go to High School, but Then Drop Out." *Catalyst* 12, no. 9 (June 2001).

11

Ending Social Promotion:
A Signature Reform

G. Alfred Hess Jr.

As director of the Center for Urban School Policy at Northwestern University, G. Alfred Hess Jr. is one of the most prominent experts on school reform in Chicago. His work has covered both citywide school reform initiatives and a special focus on high school redesign.

One of the most controversial policies implemented during the past eight years is the policy designed to stop passing along failing students to the next grade. Since 1997, this policy has resulted in the retention of between 10,000 and 14,000 students per year in the Chicago Public Schools (CPS) and led to an extended and ongoing national debate over its effects. But, despite the vocal opposition of some CPS staff and reformers, as well as research suggesting that retention somewhat increases dropout rates among those retained, the policy remains in place to the present.

Paul Vallas came to CPS in 1995 believing in the mayor's political rhetoric of getting the schools back to the basics, only promoting students if they showed they were learning, and establishing adult accountability for the successes and failures of the city's schools. Ending social promotion was at the center of the resulting policies. It is primarily a policy that relies on the threat of retention to motivate students to work harder in school and to achieve at higher levels. As first implemented, promotion gates were established at the 3rd, 6th, and 8th grades, with scores on the district's standardized reading and math tests establishing the standards for promotion. Students reading a full grade level below the national norm in 3rd grade and a year and a half below the national norm in 6th and 8th grade were subject to the retention policy.

In 1997, the first year of the program, some 27,000 students—37 percent of the district's 3rd, 6th, and 8th graders—failed to make the required "cut" scores during the spring testing on the Iowa Test of Basic Skills (ITBS). These students were mandated to attend six weeks of summer school (called "the summer bridge") and given a second chance to score above the retention cut score. Of these, about 16,000 did not pass the second administration of the ITBS at the appropriate grade. However, more than 5,000 students were waived on to the next grade; individual students could be promoted despite not achieving the required standardized test score on the recommendation of teachers and principals. In the end, 10,883 students (12.4% of 3rd, 6th, and 8th graders) were retained in the first year's implementation of the policy; nearly half of these students were in the 3rd grade. In August 1998, the second year under the policy, 12,354 were retained; in 1999

10,560 were kept back. Retention rates fell sharply in 2000 to 7,196 (7.7% of students in the tested grades).

The student retention program stayed largely intact through its first three years, except that the promotion cut score was raised by about two months each year. However, in 2000 the policy underwent more significant modifications. New systemwide criteria for waiving students were established for students in a specified range around each grade's cut score, and teachers and principals were given more control of this waiver process. The number of students retained, 7,225, was similar to the prior year's total. In 2001–2002, the district shifted away from using grade equivalents for its test reporting to using scale scores, which had the effect of raising the passing score and resulted in a jump in the number of students retained to 11,155. For technical reasons in scoring the test, the number retained dropped below 10,000 students in 2003.

To some extent, these changes were the result of loud and persistent opposition to the program. Don Moore of the school reform group Designs for Change and Julie Woestehoff of Parents United for Responsible Education (PURE) have been consistently vocal opponents of the policy. Moore has enlisted nationally renowned testing experts such as Robert Hauser, chair of a National Research Council panel on the appropriate uses of testing, to issue sharp criticisms of the policy. In particular, educators nationwide have criticized the use of a single test score to make decisions about students' educational paths, because an individual's test scores can vary significantly from one test administration to the next. Giving students two chances to pass the test somewhat mitigates this problem, and adding a waiver range at the discretion of teachers and principals was a further attempt to respond to criticisms of the policy.

But ending social promotion was not simply a "get tough with students" policy, as it has been frequently misunderstood outside of Chicago, nor did it stand alone. Ending social promotion has to be seen as a companion policy to the establishment of school accountability that focused on standards of success for school faculties, principals, and teachers. In the political debates leading up to the mayor's takeover of the school system, teachers and their representatives had been quick to make the point that they could be excellent teachers, but if students chose not to learn, they (the teachers) should not be held accountable for the lack of student learning. By establishing an accountability system for students and threatening sanctions, Vallas was seeking to motivate not only students, but also principals and teachers, to improve their performance. This dual intent for ending the social promotion policy is frequently ignored by its opponents and is rarely considered in evaluating the effectiveness of the policy.

At the same time, the district also implemented a series of measures to support students in achieving at higher levels. Afterschool tutoring and nutrition programs were provided in the schools with the highest concentrations of lower performing students. Students who were retained were supposed to be given accelerated instruction in the following year and offered yet another opportunity to rejoin their former cohort halfway through that year, but most retained students simply repeated the previous grade level. An additional 9th-grade "gate" through which students had to pass was attempted in the first year, but quickly abandoned. While Chicago has experimented with mandatory common end-of-semester exams in 11 subjects and now utilizes the state's Prairie State Achievement Exam in 11th grade, it has no exit or graduation exam like those adopted in other places.

The impact of ending social promotion on student achievement has been neither as destructive as some opponents predicted nor as miraculous as Vallas and others hoped. Melissa Roderick and her colleagues at the Consortium on Chicago School Research, who have done the most extensive research on its effects, have found that a number of students who had been performing at levels below the established cut scores improved their achievement under threat of retention, and that passing rates for students improved during the first three years of the policy's implementation. However, they also found that students who were actually held back under the policy did not improve measurably as a result of the policy, and that one-third of the retained 8th graders were no longer in the school system two years later, underscoring the nationally documented findings that retained students were more likely to drop out than were those who had been socially promoted. Thus, the policy seems to be having its intended effect on a large number of previously lower performing students who improved their achievement levels, but has not proved beneficial for most of those who were retained.

But what of the larger effects of the policy on the effort to improve learning in Chicago's elementary schools? Under school-level accountability measures, school faculties are measured by the achievement levels of their students, specifically for the percentage of their students who achieve at or above the national norm (the median) for each grade from 3rd to 8th. Notice that the thrusts of the two policies are aimed toward different groups of students. The effort at ending social promotion focuses on the district's lowest performing students. The school accountability policies focus on moving large numbers of students from moderately low performance to above the national median at each grade. And yet the results of this two-pronged effort have been quite remarkable, with the percentage of students at or above the national norm rising from 26.5 percent in reading in 1995 to 37.6 percent in 2001, Vallas' final year. In math, the improvement was from 29.8 percent in 1995 to 43.5 percent in 2001. Improved achievement has continued under the successor administration of CEO Arne Duncan.

Ending social promotion as a companion to school accountability policies, and the support for improvement provided through both policies, has been an important component of a systemwide change in the culture of public education in Chicago. In 1995 and earlier, the focus had been on explaining why Chicago students could not be expected to perform at levels comparable with other students across the country (poverty, minority status, poor parental support for students). By 2001, the culture in the school system was firmly focused on improving student learning, and excuses for low student performance were not acceptable. Attention had shifted to thinking about the kinds of support teachers would need to dramatically improve their instruction and away from questioning whether Chicago students could learn what other students across the country were learning. Three years after Vallas' departure, a new hope for public education allows the political debate to focus on the best means to improve schools rather than on threats to dismantle the system as a means to motivate students, teachers, and principals.

12

Forget Governance: Build Capacity

Richard F. Elmore

As professor of educational leadership at the Harvard Graduate School of Education and a senior research fellow with the Consortium for Policy Research, Richard F. Elmore's research focuses on how schools in different policy contexts develop a sense of accountability and a capacity to deliver high-quality instruction. His work on school choice, school restructuring, and professional development has influenced state, local, and federal education policy for two decades.

C hicago has, for the past 15 years, been a laboratory for a number of major currents of educational reform. Most notable among them have been the dramatic shifts in organizational structures—from centralization, to decentralization, and back again. What all too often gets lost in this constant tussle is that organizational and governance changes do not, by themselves, cause people to get smarter and more effective in their work. The way to do that is to invest directly in the knowledge and skill of the teachers and administrators themselves, and to adopt a differential system in which controls on schools are tighter or looser, depending on performance.

The initial 1988 reform law was a powerfully decentralizing force—powerfully antibureaucratic and antiprofessional in its roots, heavily focused on harnessing parent and community involvement to the improvement of neighborhood schools—based on the theory that increasing direct accountability between schools and their neighborhood constituencies would enhance respect and engagement between teachers and students and eventually improve academic performance.

The effects of these decentralizing reforms is, by now, quite predictable, although we seem to have to rediscover these predictable effects with each cycle of centralization and decentralization. I have come to think of this effect as "the rule of thirds." About a third of the units receiving substantial new authority figure out how to use it in accord with policymakers' objectives; that is, they actually engage in the kind of improvement that the theory of the intervention predicts. Another third engage in what might be called "compliance behavior." They mimic the form of restructuring without engaging its substance. A final third either don't engage the reform at all or deliberately subvert it for their own ends. In fact, the rule of thirds—more politely stated—was the dominant finding of the Consortium for Chicago School Research in its studies of the early effects of the school reform law.

More importantly, however, the 1988 reform embodied the central pathology of all structural reforms during this period: It assumed that school improvement would follow naturally from changing the organizational and governance structure within which schools operate. We probably knew at the time, and we certainly know now, that this theory is at best incomplete, and at worst flatly wrong. The central problem of school performance is that most teachers and administrators literally don't know what to do to improve the academic work of students. Changing the organizational and governance structure around their practice simply means that they don't know what to do in a different structure; it doesn't change the state of their knowledge and skill.

The Vallas era is generally characterized as cleaning up and rationalizing the bureaucratic structure, as well as a period of recentralization. Instructionally, however, they were not great years. In fact, the lack of clarity and coherence in the system around instructional issues actually increased with the introduction of multiple comprehensive school reform models in failing schools. On top of the LSC governance structure, this Chinese menu approach to school improvement (one from column A, one from column B) reinforced the view that it didn't so much matter what instructional practice schools pursued as long as someone somewhere was paying attention to it.

With the present phase of reform, Chicago has finally come to terms with the problems of large-scale school improvement of academic instruction. The appointment of a strong chief academic officer, the creation of subunits charged with instructional improvement, the appointment of area instructional officers with responsibility for working directly with principals and schools on instructional issues, the creation of a professional development plan, a focus on instructional improvement in reading and mathematics, and an accountability structure that evaluates and rewards principals and teachers for participating in professional development and instructional improvement work—all of these aspects of the district's education plan point toward a serious systemic commitment, finally, to instructional improvement.

The education plan is fully developed, but it is in the early stages of implementation. As we say in the policy analysis business, paraphrasing von Clausewitz, implementation is the continuation of policymaking by other means. Whether the system is able to make this transition from structure, governance, and generic management to a focus on instructional improvement depends on how well it will address the following problems:

1. The Residue of Previous Reforms

In keeping with the great tradition of urban school reform, Chicago has not replaced one reform strategy with another. It has, in fact, layered a new reform strategy on top of the accumulated residue of earlier reforms. At the ground level in many schools, the old structure still is the governance structure, no matter what the system says the new structure is.

2. The Problem of Scale

Simply put, no one has done instructional improvement on the scale that it has to be done in Chicago. The issues of scale are multiple: Large-scale instructional improvement strategies, like land wars, succeed or fail by the number of feet on the ground. Large numbers of people have to be in schools and classrooms working directly with teachers and principals in order to raise the level of instructional practice. More importantly, the people who work in schools have to be engaged in a common agenda, they have to have a common conception of their work, and they have to be given the authority to raise questions about aspects of the strategy that are not working on the ground. This kind of change cannot be done by bureaucratic mandate. It has to be done in face-to-face relations between people who introduce the new culture and people who are expected to learn it and incorporate it into their practice.

3. The Inevitable Slide toward Incoherence

Changing the culture of large-scale systems like Chicago requires relentless focus, consistency, and persistence on the part of senior leaders. At the same time, it also requires the gradual construction of greater and greater depth of understanding among principals and teacher leaders so they ultimately learn to take over the work of instructional improvement. Ultimately, it becomes the job of the system to respond to the demands of schools for the resources and knowledge necessary to pursue improvement. Without thoughtful, strategic planning, professional development can slide in the direction of incoherence, either because schools are demanding things that aren't on the systems agenda, or the system is providing things that don't help schools improve.

4. The Big-Endians versus the Little-Endians

In Jonathan Swift's *Gulliver's Travels*, Gulliver at one point comes in contact with a society that is engaged in an endless, detailed, excruciatingly dull and detailed, highly conflictual debate about whether, in eating a soft-boiled egg, one should first crack the big end or the little end. This devastating parody of religious orthodoxy applies to the tiresome and increasingly meaningless debate over centralization and decentralization in educational systems. The evidence from several generations of centralization and decentralization suggests that the answer to the question "Should we centralize or decentralize?" is an emphatic and resounding "yes." That is, in a performance-based accountability system, the authority to exercise discretion over instructional practice should have to be earned by exemplary performance, and those who are exemplary performers have an obligation to acknowledge the rewards of increased discretion by working with colleagues in lower-performing schools. Likewise, schools that cannot demonstrate adequate performance should not exercise discretion or control over instructional practice and they should have to engage in a deliberate process of improvement.

In addressing these challenges, Chicago has several advantages. Mayor Richard M. Daley brings enormous tactical and strategic skill to the problem of how to reconcile political localism with the demands for systemic improvement. Schools CEO Arne Duncan has the political authority to push hard on accountability issues. Based on recent research showing that schools that are successful at instructional improvement are schools that create a strong normative environment around instructional practice, the system is moving from the expectation that these schools are the exception to the expectation that they will be the rule.

And yet, serious obstacles remain. The current directory of professional development opportunities in Chicago reads more like the menu of an all-you-can-eat buffet than like a carefully crafted meal at a four-star restaurant. One has the sense that quantity has won out, in the short term, over quality. At the same time, it remains unclear whether Chicago is ready to adopt differential treatment toward schools in which accountability is tight on performance and loose on practice for high-performing schools, and those where it is tight on performance and tight on practice for low-performing schools.

Most of all, the problem is that Chicago has been mired for at least 15 years, and probably more like a century, in the pointless political discourse of centralization and decentralization, much like Gulliver's big-endians and little-endians. Everybody talks the language of centralization and decentralization even though it has long since ceased to have any useful application to the actual problems of school improvement in Chicago. Part of the cultural change necessary in Chicago is a change in political discourse, away from the idea that there is something inherently good or bad about the transfer of authority from one level of the system to another, toward the idea that how much authority and discretion you exercise should be a function of how good you are at what you do.

13

A View from Pershing Road

Timothy D. Brandhorst

Timothy D. Brandhorst, an attorney, served in the city of Chicago's law department, then moved to the Chicago Public Schools shortly after the mayoral takeover in 1995. He was director of labor relations and, later, director of policy development. He now works for the American Bar Association.

B y the time the state legislature granted Mayor Richard M. Daley control of the Chicago Public Schools (CPS), he had been mayor for eight years, and many in his administration had settled into middle management assignments with little hope of rapid upward progress. Consequently, schools CEO Paul Vallas and Board of Education president Gery Chico had no problem recruiting scores of ambitious lawyers, managers, and analysts from city departments to administer the school system.

Vallas brought his top assistants from the city's budget office, mostly twenty-something budget analysts and lawyers, the kind of young politicos who dream of one day running a city department or being the mayor's chief of staff. Vallas spread his people throughout the Pershing Road bureaucracy—in finance, human resources, the budget office, benefits, operations, technology. They were the tentacles of the Vallas octopus, an independent network with all lines leading back to Paul.

The new crew faced, first, the massive and decrepit Pershing Road facility: three enormous brick buildings connected by walkways, extending a third of a mile down the block from the old meatpacking district, isolated from the schools, teachers, principals, parents, students. Of the 45,000 CPS employees, fewer than 1,500 worked in this fortress; the building could have held five times that many. Instead, as workers slowly expanded into their surroundings over the decades, it had absorbed mounds of files, reports, and paper.

For the new team, it was like walking into a paper jungle. Massive desks and tables (handmade by CPS carpenters) sat on torn, stained carpeting. Water leaked through the ceilings; one worker simply kept her small potted tree underneath the spot where rainwater dripped down into her office. The afternoon sun overpowered the ancient HVAC, baking those with west-facing windows. On hot days, the pungent tang drifting down the block from the old slaughterhouses mixed with stale air wafting up the stairwells from the basements (rumored to have served as cavalry stables during World War I).

Those basements were like dungeons, a jumbled maze of hundreds of sealed storage rooms. Each division within each department kept possession of its own room or rooms, with its own lock and key; most hadn't been opened in years. Entering one of these was like opening a time capsule. Broken lamps and chairs and desks and shelves were piled high atop file cabinets holding employee work records dating back decades. Rain fell through broken ceiling-level windows onto 1930s-era student attendance records.

One of the Vallas team's first acts, in September 1995, was to lay off over a thousand of the union trade workers—carpenters, plumbers, electricians, etc.—who occupied the first-floor CPS shop. The first layoff came swiftly. Even three years later, when CPS left Pershing Road and moved its offices downtown, the shops still smelled of grease and cigarette smoke, and still held evidence of workers taken by surprise the day of their layoff: a spoon stuck in a cup of yogurt in the metal shop, half a can of Coke on that day's sports page, a to-do list of repairs to be made at a school.

I joined the Vallas team some nine months after the layoffs began. On my third day of work, I faced a roomful of typographical workers—the men and women of the district's print shop, all of whom were laid off when their printing work was privatized. They weren't angry—they seemed to know that they weren't really needed, and that surely they would be able to find work elsewhere in union print shops. Rather, I was struck by what concerned them most: what we were going to do with their machinery.

They spoke eloquently about saving their printing equipment, about making sure the equipment found a good home, as if the machines were flesh and blood. It was as if they knew that things at CPS had to change, and they accepted the layoff as part of that fundamental change—but they wanted to make sure we took care of their old friends, the printing presses. (As it turned out, the equipment was already obsolete.)

There followed a steady series of smaller layoffs of central office workers through mid-1997. Many in the bureaucracy had worked there for years, even decades, had seen a number of new superintendents come and go, and, at first, expected to be able to keep their heads down and wait out the new regime. But the 1995 legislation that transferred control to the mayor also eliminated civil service protections against layoff for all nonteaching employees, and it soon became apparent that the administration wouldn't tolerate reluctance to change. It seemed there was another round of layoffs every month. Drip, drip, drip: one person from this department, two from another, a handful at a time.

Morale fell through the floor. But by 1997 Chico and Vallas had balanced the budget and had the attention of the traditionally sluggish and contentious central office staff.

Vallas' new team installed a pair of large, do-it-yourself coffee urns holding Starbucks coffee in one corner of the cafeteria, with a stack of Starbucks cups and lids. The new Vallas recruits carried their Starbucks cups like badges of honor. The cups became symbolic, the shorthand some in the old guard used to dismissively describe the Vallas people and the totem the new team used to mark membership in their tribe. The new recruits carried their Starbucks cups, walked fast, met only behind closed doors, and scared the hell out of everyone else.

The feeling among those on Vallas' team was, we can do no wrong, because we can't possibly screw things up any worse than they already are. We could just look around the building and get a sense of how badly decayed and rotted the system was.

In the first couple of years, everything happened unbelievably quickly. An idea in Paul's brain could blossom into a funded, complex program within a few weeks or months. Kids can't learn because they can't see the chalkboard? Within months Paul got tens of thousands of pairs of eyeglasses donated to the district and distributed to the children. Teachers line the halls every payday because the antiquated computer system can't calculate their checks right? Within weeks, a special payroll service center went up outside the building to help employees resolve pay issues quickly. The engineers union consists of middle-aged white males? Paul insisted that the union implement an apprenticeship program, hire only recent CPS graduates, or face layoff and privatization; within a few months the apprentices had been hired. Test scores at a handful of schools have dropped two years in a row? Paul demanded a plan to reconstitute those schools, and within a few months it had been implemented.

Vallas and Chico have always downplayed the extent of their rivalry during their time at CPS, usually spinning their intense differences as no more than a healthy intellectual debate between two men who care deeply about the children of Chicago. The truth was that most of the managers under them remained loyal to whichever one had recruited them. You were either with Paul or you were with Gery. It was that simple. Every action was calibrated by how it might be received from the head of the opposing camp.

Day-to-day, the CPS world revolved around Vallas. Chico, as president of the Board of Trustees, was physically present just three days each month: at the Board meeting itself, on media day, and, one week before the Board meeting, his bravura "President's briefing." It was because of the last that Chico had his greatest impact internally. Late into the night, Chico grilled the senior managers from every corner of the organization over every point of policy to come before the Board. It made Chico a constant, looming psychological presence in the minds of the system's managers.

But the rest of the month Vallas was there early, stayed late, and, like a power plant, energized the building every moment of every day. An enormous, ornate desk that had been the throne of his predecessor sat at one end of his long office. Paul refused to sit at it, symbolically rejecting the trappings of the office, and instead used the long conference table that filled the rest of the room as his workspace. Behind him, a window ran the length of the room. Through the window, miles to the northeast, the Loop skyline (and City Hall) shimmered Oz-like in the sun and haze.

Paul kept stacks of memos and correspondence in the middle of the table, and during meetings would inevitably multitask, listening to the discussion while reading (or, frequently, while talking to a reporter). Meetings were held back-to-back around this conference table, and often spilled into one another as his top 15 or 20 advisors weighed in on multiple issues.

Of course, as the dust settled, the sense of excitement wore off. The structures we put into place stabilized the school system, but also gradually stabilized the CPS bureaucracy; even Vallas' bright eager inner circle began to ossify. The CPS central offices left the massive Pershing Road fortress for a Loop office building in 1998, and even the physical surroundings were suddenly normal. By 2000, that first period—those heady first weeks and months of the Vallas administration—seemed like a dream. There's been nothing like it since.

14

Missing in Action:
The Chicago Teachers Union

Linda Lenz

Linda Lenz is a journalist who has covered the Chicago Public Schools for 25 years, first at the Chicago Sun-Times *and then at* Catalyst, *a nonprofit newsmagazine she founded that is published by the Community Renewal Society.*

In September 1987, as the striking Chicago Teachers Union (CTU) was heading for what would end up being a prolonged walkout, a prominent civic leader remarked privately that he hoped the strike would drag on a bit longer. Maybe then, he reasoned, public fury would rise to the point where politicians finally would be compelled to shake up the ossified school system.

He was right. The union's ninth and longest strike in 18 years lit the fuse for school reform in Chicago. Within a year of that 17-day work stoppage, the Illinois General Assembly passed legislation that created elected local school councils (LSCs) and gave them significant powers, including the hiring and firing of principals.

The union and its leadership emerged from this upheaval virtually untouched, which is not surprising, given the union's sizeable campaign contributions. In the 14 years that followed, the decisions of the CTU's old-guard leadership continued to fuel reforms, sometimes unwittingly, and sometimes in ways that worked against their traditional interests. Only recently has this dynamic begun to change.

In the years leading to the 1987 strike, Chicago had become ripe for school reform. Research and advocacy groups won front-page headlines with studies of academic failure and bureaucratic mismanagement. Shooting their arrows at the school administration rather than the union, these groups followed up with proposals to reshape the system, largely by pushing more authority down to the school level. Siding with the activists, the teachers union chimed in with a proposal for school-site management that gave teachers a bigger voice.

In addition to these efforts, there was a key shift in the political landscape. For the first time the city had a mayor with a demonstrated concern for the city's schoolchildren. In 1986, Mayor Harold Washington convened a closed-door "summit" of education, business, and civic leaders to craft a plan to improve education. However, the school superintendent, Manford Byrd Jr., insisted that little could be done without more money, and the work of the summit ground to a halt.

Then came the strike.

Education and community groups seized on the teachers' walkout to organize parents throughout the city. Rich and poor, black, brown, and white, parents rallied to end the strike and improve the system. "I'd been waiting for this opportunity for 20 years," teacher activist Bernie Noven told writer Mary O'Connell for her cogent analysis of those days. (See "School Reform Chicago Style: How Citizens Organized to Change Public Policy," a report published in 1991 by the Center for Neighborhood Technology.)

The uproar pushed Washington off his original decision to remain uninvolved in the contract talks. He forced the School Board to accept a settlement that tilted toward the union and gave him an opening to press for systemwide change, and he revived and expanded his summit, adding parents and community representatives. His charge to the rejuvenated body was to reach consensus on how to improve the system. That work had barely begun when Washington died suddenly of a heart attack.

The broad-based summit, which included the teachers union, reached an official consensus that centered on program expansion—for example, more preschool classrooms—rather than fundamental change, such as school-site management. But this was not enough for the business and community representatives, who bolted from the summit and eventually carried the day with the state legislature, focusing on decentralization rather than additional funding and programs.

Equally fed up with the status quo, the teachers union did not object to the business leaders' push for decentralization. In the end, the union suffered only two losses: one, teachers would have only two seats on each 11-member local school council—the union had pushed for more; and two, principals henceforth would be able to fill teacher vacancies without regard to seniority.

Despite these changes, however, financial and academic problems still continued after 1988, prolonging the feeling of uncertainty. The Board of Education appointed by the city's new mayor, Richard M. Daley, got off to a great start with the union by approving raises of 21 percent over three years. Meant to buy labor peace, the contract wreaked havoc instead because revenue repeatedly fell short of projections.

These revenue problems triggered a string of school budget cuts and patchwork solutions as the union, forced back into negotiations by an escape clause in the contract, fought hard to preserve what it could of that three-year deal and then to make up lost ground in subsequent contracts. As September approached each year, no one knew whether schools would open on time. In some years, when teachers returned to work without a new contract, it appeared as though they might close after they had opened.

While this labor unrest never resulted in a strike, it did feed into a second major course correction in reform. Coupled with slower than expected progress on test scores, the school system's continuing financial and labor difficulties set the corporate community on a new school mission: getting the mayor to take responsibility for the school system. In modern-day Chicago, the mayor has always appointed the School Board. However, the decentralization legislation of 1988 created a grassroots nominating process that tied his hands and gave him candidates he didn't want. The mayor acceded to the corporate community's pleas.

Taking advantage of a historic Republican takeover of the state legislature and the governor's office in 1994, Chicago's Democratic mayor worked behind the scenes with the opposition to overhaul the system once again. Local school councils remained in place, but the mayor got unfettered authority to name a slimmed-down School Board and appoint a chief executive officer. He also got a number of financial restrictions removed, allowing his school team to start off with an immediate, impressive hat trick: approving a secure four-year teachers' contract, mounting new programs, and putting the school system on firm financial ground.

As icing on the cake, the GOP stripped Chicago's school unions of the power to negotiate over such workplace issues as class size, layoff procedures, and privatization. However, Daley's handpicked school leadership team did not walk through that door. Rather, to maintain peace with the Chicago Teachers Union, a major financial backer of Democratic candidates, the new school leaders retained contractual workplace rules as a matter of policy.

Daley's team did take advantage of another change that took place: the election of Thomas Reece as the new head of the CTU. Reece, who succeeded the steely and combative Jacqueline Vaughn, was a barely engaged "go-along" guy. He rarely appeared in the press or visited schools. In return for long-term contracts with guaranteed raises, he let Vallas run the system unimpeded even by rhetoric. When Vallas abruptly reconstituted seven high schools in 1997, removing some teachers and scaring away others, the union protest was barely audible. In essence, the CTU went underground.

Much as it helped ease the way for Vallas and Chico, weak union leadership could only last so long. By 1998, high school teachers, traditionally more militant than elementary teachers, had had enough of this gentlemen's agreement. In the biennial union elections, challengers to the Reece slate swept the high school seats on the central leadership body. Reece hung on to elementary teachers, who outnumber high school teachers roughly three to one, and thus hung on to his job. But he was losing ground quickly.

Deborah Lynch-Walsh, the main challenger for leadership of the union, had worked eight years in the Washington, D.C., headquarters of the American Federation of Teachers before returning to Chicago in 1993 to run a professional development center for teachers. Devastated by the deaths of Vaughn and other allies, and discouraged by Reece's laid-back approach, she returned to the classroom in 1995. But she continued to lead, convincing teachers at her school to adopt Success For All, a demanding, nationally recognized reading program.

She also plotted a run against Reece, visiting schools to build support. After losing in both 1996 and 1998, she decided to make one last try, in 2001. By then, the teaching corps had been infused with new teachers who were prepared to try new things. And school CEO Vallas had worn out his welcome. In what was seen as a referendum against Vallas as well as Reece, Lynch-Walsh won handily. "This election was about respect and it was about dignity and it was about voice," she proclaimed on election night. School reform, the new leadership said, should be done *with* teachers, not to them.

With fortuitous timing, this union revolution came just as a new school administration was shifting the focus of reform from supplemental programs and crack-the-whip accountability to the quality of leadership and instruction.

Lynch (she dropped the Walsh) quickly brought the Chicago Teachers Union into the Teachers Union Reform Network, which promotes union-board collaboration to improve education, and revived plans for a union-run graduate program in teacher leadership. She protested loudly when current CEO Arne Duncan announced, with only an hour's notice, the closing of three schools for poor performance in the spring of 2002. She convinced Mayor Daley to drop his opposition to a bill that would restore some of the bargaining rights teachers had lost in 1995. And she got the School Board to hold off for a year on the closing of ten ineffective schools while the union helps lead change efforts at them.

Such activism augurs well for Chicago's schools. It gives teachers a way to exert leadership and stay fresh. It brings a real-world view of the classroom into decisionmaking on programs and policy. It could potentially generate peer pressure for positive change and get teachers to take some responsibility for policing their own ranks. In a city as large as Chicago, the school system needs all the leadership it can get. Even the best school administration can't get lasting improvement on its own.

15

Picking Principals:
Vallas Goes Too Far

John Ayers

As executive director of Leadership for Quality Education, a Chicago-based school reform organization affiliated with the city's business community, John Ayers has been involved in increasing the number and quality of charter schools, helping revamp the principal selection and evaluation process, and calling attention to the ongoing need to improve academic achievement for all students.

Picking the new principal of a Chicago school can be a full-contact political blood sport. As then schools chief Paul Vallas learned in 1999, trying to win authority to pick all of them is mortal combat. And, in the end, it was his undoing.

Chicago is the only large city in the United States that has decentralized so many key powers—most notably principal selection—to the community level. Each Chicago school has an

elected local school council (LSC) under the 1988 school reform law that remains largely in effect to the present. Principals, who lack tenure protections, serve the school council under a four-year contract. Together, councils and principals
have control over state and federal discretionary funding that
averages over $500,000 per school.

This concentration of power at the school level fundamentally changes the traditional balance of power between
schools and central office administrators. In theory, the Chicago setup gives little control to the Board of Education and to
district administrators. But how can a district leader improve
schools overall under these conditions?

This became one of the main challenges that schools
CEO Paul Vallas faced when he arrived in 1995. He came to
power as a result of the mayor taking control of the schools.
Vallas was not a fan of the 1988 reform; he was there to fix it.
Yet lawmakers had left most of the radical school governance
changes from 1988 in place, and simply grafted the mayor's
power to control the top jobs and to intervene in failing
schools onto the 1988 law.

Not surprisingly, Vallas sought to dominate the principal
selection game right from the start, as much as he could. The
principal selection law contained a few loopholes and limits
on LSCs' authority to appoint principals, especially where
schools were struggling or dysfunctional. Vallas used every option at his disposal to influence the process. He tied up the
LSCs with elaborate procedural plays, legal gambits, and raw
power moves whenever a principal vacancy appeared. A principal hire requires seven votes out of an LSC of ten voters, the
principal being the eleventh member. With frequent vacan-

cies, it was tough to hold seven votes when Vallas' political people were in the house and they wanted another candidate or a delay.

In public, Vallas tried to discredit LSCs wherever possible, arguing that they were standing in the way of further school improvements and too often dismissed good principals and hired questionable ones. "Goon squads" is what the reform groups called the CEO's operatives. Vallas' goal was to place loyalists in the plum jobs, and everyone knew it.

At his peak in 1999, after three years of dramatically improving test scores that were trumpeted to the hills by his energetic, self-promoting leadership style, Vallas had used his power to appoint more than 75 interim and acting principals—stop-gap arrangements put in place by central office fiat, often while LSCs sought to regain local political credibility after an attack by the hardnosed central and regional office folks. He had fired principals and disbanded councils at failing schools. Reeling from Vallas' steamrolling interventions, LSCs across the city struggled to assemble the needed votes to appoint their own choices.

But Vallas wanted even more control. And, in 1999, he finally went far beyond his mandate, and the hubris he demonstrated was his undoing.

It is worth noting that things were still going well for Vallas in 1999, after four years at the helm. Most civic leaders were willing to give Vallas the benefit of the doubt. They liked his manic energy—the organization was, for once, on its toes, trying to keep up with its active and effusive leader. The jumps in test scores were impressive. They saw the mayor's team's swinging the reform pendulum back to more central office initiative as a good thing, particularly for low-performing schools that in five years had been unable to move in a positive direction under their own power, even with considerable discretionary money. Vallas was still the new sheriff and a tough, aggressive one, to be sure, but he also appeared to be listening to a wide range of opinions. He was unpredictable, but smart and engaging.

Vallas won the trust of many powerful forces in the city, and he did so mostly by saying yes and spending lavishly in the booming mid-1990s, while at the same time projecting an image of shaping up the bureaucratic schools structure he and the mayor inherited. Black parents were impressed. In a bid to unseat Richard M. Daley in 1999's mayoral election, Congressman Bobby Rush made the main issue Vallas' leadership of the still lagging schools. The issue got no traction because polls showed black voters were impressed with Vallas' impatience with school failure. Rush failed to carry even his own ward.

However, in the spring of 1999, Vallas overstepped. His political miscalculation played out in Springfield, the dreary state capital three hours southwest of the city. Vallas had worked in the state capital for a decade in the 1980s and was seen as a proficient "numbers guy," working for the progressive Democratic comptroller Dawn Clark Netsch and the nonpartisan Economic and Fiscal Commission. In the 1990s he had become the revenue director and then budget director for Daley. Even in these fairly unexciting jobs, he grabbed headlines. A unanimous 50-0 budget vote in 1997 from the contentious city council got him branded a young political genius. Vallas felt he knew Springfield and could have his way there.

Keeping his own counsel, Vallas hatched a plan to give his CEO's office veto power over LSC principal selection. This would have been a complete gutting of the 1988 law. He had told his LSC allies that he would simply be offering a bill to seek some minor protections for principals subject to "arbitrary actions" of unfair councils—a relatively small change. But in reality he had betrayed their trust and sought much broader authority.

To be fair, there were at least a handful of instances in which LSCs appeared to have become unworkable, dysfunctional entities. Because the central office and the law department had to step in to manage these problems, Vallas and his team made the classic bureaucratic mistake and decided that councils as a whole were "a problem."

But when reform groups got wind of Vallas' aggressive legislative attack, a large and impressive mobilization got quickly under way. Remarkably, Vallas did not back down one bit, even when his own followers urged him to withdraw or soften the proposal. Vallas, ever the legislative poker player, voiced confidence that legislators would see it his way in the end. He hinted that the mayor, who shared his concern about principals being treated unfairly, would support his legislation and win the day. The principals' association outwardly supported the change, but whispered that Vallas may have gone too far with this one.

Yet reform leaders who wanted to preserve the authority of the LSCs feared Vallas was not bluffing. And, in the end, they found an ally from an unexpected source. When the mayor appointed Vallas in 1995, he also selected a small, business-dominated board chaired by his former chief of staff, Gery Chico.

A glib attorney, Chico was Vallas' constant rival for attention and credit. By 1999 he had grown tired of Vallas' grandstanding style. His role on the mayor's team was that of the accommodator, the man who sat for hours at public comment sessions listening respectfully to community complaints and concerns about the schools. He and his fellow Board members would regularly turn to Paul Vallas asking, "What are we doing about that?" Vallas would rattle off half a dozen initiatives from his huge catalogue of ideas—some real, some imagined, many half-baked.

In this process, Chico had grown to know and like some LSC leaders and reformers. He recognized their legitimate role in advancing reform. He began to see Vallas more and more as an apologist for the system and a self-serving braggart. Speculation is that Chico found Vallas' 1999 Springfield play to rout the 1988 reforms a risky and unnecessary grab for personal power, and his finely honed political sense was that it would be seen as such by legitimate community leaders.

Vallas' tactic came undone that spring when two things happened: 1) the mayor's powerful Springfield lobbyists refused to enter the fray, and 2) the existing LSCs raised a massive outcry against the Vallas initiative that impacted legislators' view. The jig was up. No one knows for sure, but Chico probably advised the mayor's political staff to stay clear of the controversy as the community campaign to stop the legislation picked up.

In the end, business leaders helped create a compromise that allowed arbitration in cases of arbitrary action against principals with satisfactory ratings, but also called for the re-vamping of principal evaluation procedures. Powerful Hyde Park Representative Barbara Flynn Currie, the sponsor of Vallas' original bill, stated on the House floor, "What is different in this legislation from the original is [that] the balance of power between Vallas and the LSCs remains untouched."

Noticed by few at the time, this debacle showed the first chinks in Vallas' armor. It also began to reveal the deepening rift with Chico. The two men began to jealously seek the public's and the mayor's attention on school policy, and bad policy began to result—Vallas created a teacher preparation academy, Chico sought federal funds and built a bigger one of his own. The test scores flattened out, and Vallas' own bureaucracy and cronyism became more apparent. In the spring of 2001, two years after the Springfield overreach, the mayor sought and got the resignation of both Chico and Vallas.

16

Beefing Up Professional Development

Alexander Russo

Chicago Public Schools (CPS) professional development czar Al Bertani likens himself to Tom Ridge, President Bush's Homeland Security chief. Like Ridge, Bertani has been given the enormous responsibility of overseeing what has become a top-priority initiative: Chicago's effort to help classroom teachers and principals become more effective. Like Ridge, Bertani's portfolio has been expanded across several disparate offices. And yet, like Ridge, Bertani doesn't have control over many parts of the $123 million–plus bureaucracy that he is supposed to direct.

Even with these challenges, recent developments have made it clear that attitudes toward professional development are slowly changing in Chicago. After nearly 15 years of focusing on governance and accountability strategies, the current administration under schools chief Arne Duncan seems to have woken up to the idea that school reform is eventually bound to stall without significant investment in the development of its teachers and school leaders. The new approach, which some insiders have already named the "third wave" of school reform in Chicago, seeks to balance previous efforts that emphasized such things as decentralization and testing with a more instructional, human resources perspective. So far, this effort includes staff changes, increased professional development offerings, the placement of school-based reading specialists, and a shift in budget priorities.

However, as highlighted by a just-completed inventory of professional development spending at the district and school levels, a daunting series of organizational, cultural, and financial changes lie ahead. This early in the process, it is still unclear whether Chicago's "turnaround" on professional development will be sustained or successful.

A FRAGMENTED HISTORY

Like many other large urban school systems, Chicago's previous efforts at professional development have often been characterized as fragmented, incoherent, inconsistent, and ineffective. "In the past, there was no accountability for professional development," says Chicago Public Education Fund president Janet Knupp, whose organization helped produce the 2002 inventory of professional development spending in Chicago. Citing lack of standards for instruction and training, as well as poor coordination among various parts of the district bureaucracy, Knupp says, "The strategy was to have no strategy."

According to Knupp and many others, staff development at the district level had been—as it is in many large urban districts—inconsistent and ineffective. There had been no clear focus on any particular academic area, instructional model, or grade level. Most support programs had provided no more than one day per week of on-site assistance. Professional development functions had been scattered throughout the bureaucracy, hidden in various line items.

In fact, a series of earlier reports had long suggested problems with professional development. Though never widely released, a 1997 study by the consulting firm KPMG Peat Marwick found that "a sustained, comprehensive, system-wide devotion to provide teacher development and support does not exist." Also, according to a survey of teachers published last year by the Consortium on Chicago School Research, professional development in the city has been "largely a fragmented and individualistic activity."

Surveyed in 1997 and 1999, Chicago teachers reported experiencing some form of professional development two to three times a month, usually within their schools. The 2001 report noted that fewer teachers reported being "left on their own" to seek out opportunities, but researchers still found significant variations in the amount and quality of professional development among different types of schools—and even among different types of teachers within the same school.

A LACK OF RELEVANCE

Perhaps most obvious of all, Chicago's districtwide professional development and institute days have provided no coherent focus to teachers, and have often not been closely relevant to their work. In 2001–2002, the district spent $56 million on eight such inservice days—roughly $7 million per day. "Basically, half of the money spent on professional development at the district level is used for these days," says Knupp, one of many critics of how the days have been used in the past. "One of them is used as Teacher Appreciation Day."

That's an expensive form of teacher appreciation, and not necessarily the kind of appreciation overworked and underpaid teachers want. However, lacking any coherent direction or support from the district, principals and classroom teachers in Chicago were largely left on their own to find and develop professional development programs. Individual schools were not always able to make effective decisions about professional development, coordinate multiple efforts, or even make use of the money budgeted for that purpose. One Chicago expert claimed that 35 percent of school-based professional development funds went unspent each year.

External efforts to support teachers have been similarly flawed. The city's $5 million "external partner" program gives individual schools a choice to work with one of several universities and outside organizations, but is limited to a small set of roughly 100 schools that are on academic probation, out of nearly 600 schools in the district. Such partnerships can often revitalize professional development efforts by offering fresh thinking and "outsider" perspectives. But Chicago's external partner program doesn't provide the intense, ongoing support for classroom teachers that most experts now recommend. For $50,000 to $100,000 per school, most external partners have had staff on site for only one day a week. The quality of the assistance has varied tremendously, by most accounts. "The problem with external partners is that they have external agendas," says Dave Peterson of the Chicago Principals and Administrators Association, "not the least of which is getting additional schools to hire them as consultants."

By many accounts, lack of leadership from the top was for many years a key part of the problem. "[Paul Vallas, the schools' former CEO,] didn't understand professional development," says Liz Duffrin, a senior editor at *Catalyst*, an independent education magazine published in Chicago. "He had a different attitude toward teachers, and Chicago was in a different place when he first arrived [in 1995]. He came in to crack the whip on accountability and sort out the district's finances, and for a long time they were getting results with the things they were doing." Duffrin also points out that professional development was much less popular as a reform issue nine years ago than it is today.

THE BEGINNINGS OF CHANGE

Only when annual reading scores flattened out and Vallas left in 2001 did things really start to change in Chicago, in terms of staffing and priorities. Many observers cite the hiring of strong education leaders in prominent positions as the most obvious signals. New schools chief Arne Duncan brought in a strong educational leader in Barbara Eason-Watkins, a former elementary school principal, and gave her wide authority. In turn, Eason-Watkins appointed Al Bertani, who had run an admired principal training program for the Chicago Principals Association, and hired Tim Shanahan, a nationally prominent reading expert, to design and head a new reading initiative.

Begun in 2001–2002, the reading initiative initially gave 114 of the lowest-performing elementary schools full-time reading specialists as coaches for classroom teachers, a $12 million program paid for by the district. Summer programs were also expanded. Starting in the summer of 2002, roughly 1,200 teachers, representing more than 300 schools, received 60 hours of training. The district also provided eight half-days of staff development to teams from 67 of 77 high schools over the summer, with plans for eight additional sessions during the school year. Since then, CPS has been steadily increasing the number of site-based reading specialists and hiring reading coaches for each instructional area to support school-based activities.

There are other small, but nonetheless important, signs of change in Chicago. Historically thought of as hostile to outside reform efforts, the district became one of the first sites in the nation to participate in New Leaders for New Schools, an innovative principal training program modeled after Teach For America. The Chicago Teachers Union, also under new leadership, started a new school for the development of teacher leadership, the Urban School Leadership Academy; celebrated its tenth year running the Quest Center, a much-heralded professional development initiative; and is partnering with CPS to revamp the academic program at ten particularly troubled schools.

Looking back, observers consider Chicago's first few months under these new initiatives a qualified success. Reading scores were among the highest ever in 2002 and, while some scores dipped in 2003, results on state measures showed continued progress. Just as important, opposition from teachers and principals has been minimal thus far. To some extent, changes of leadership at CPS and the teachers union have helped to ease the way. An influx of increased federal funds over the past two years has softened the blow of state budget cuts and is paying for much of the expansion. In addition, Duncan and his team have taken a much less critical attitude toward schools and teachers, many of whom felt that Vallas unfairly blamed them for everything.

Flexibility has also been key, according to reading program designer Shanahan, who contrasts Chicago's approach with more prescriptive efforts in Los Angeles and a bigger emphasis on monitoring teachers in San Diego. "In Los Angeles, everyone has to use Open Court [a phonics-based reading program]," says Shanahan. "In San Diego, the coach is really there to make sure that you do what you're supposed to do." While his program does require some specific practices, such as a certain amount of phonics instruction, Shanahan believes in giving educators a fair amount of freedom. "A lot of things work," he says. "You don't mandate something just for the sake of control."

CHALLENGES REMAIN

Despite the early progress, significant challenges remain. For starters, CPS has yet to address the issue of revamping the use of the eight current professional development days, having failed to make substantial changes in the latest union contract. Salary increments for college credits, advanced degrees, and national certification are another issue that has been left unaddressed, even though such pay raises cost CPS an estimated $47 million per year.

In addition, not everyone has been satisfied with the changes that have taken place in the name of professional development. Unhappy with the reassignment of his office under the aegis of the professional development unit—it was previously a separate content area department—Shanahan returned to the University of Illinois at Chicago before the start of school in 2002 after just one year on the job. And Bertani still lacks direct control over 23 of the 40-odd offices that provide professional development in the CPS bureaucracy. "I have pass-through authority," says Bertani of his current portfolio. "But I'm essentially coordinating among multiple agencies." Most important, the extent to which there have been actual changes in professional development at the school level remains unclear. Besides expanded summer offerings, few if any concrete reallocations have been made thus far to the $28 million spent on individual professional development for teachers and principals or the $39 million spent on school-focused efforts.

While the 57-page CPS education plan for 2002 includes explicit frameworks for high-quality teaching and professional development, no one knows how extensively—if at all—it is being used in the field. The system is still a long way from being able to demonstrate any impact on achievement from its efforts.

As in other cities, revamping professional development in Chicago is proving to be complex, delicate, and not particularly glamorous work. So far, things seem to have gone better in Chicago than in some other places, such as San Diego, where professional development has been extremely contentious. But the easiest steps—studying the problem, reorganizing, and hiring good central office people—can only get you so far. The most important parts, including the work of the 200-plus reading specialists and substantive changes to how schools schedule and provide professional development, will come much more slowly.

This article originally appeared in the Harvard Education Letter *(November/December 2002).*

FOR FURTHER INFORMATION

Catalyst featured Chicago's new professional development efforts in its June 2002 issue. Available online at www.catalyst-chicago.org/06-02/0602toc.htm

Also see *Catalyst's* October 2001 issue on National Board certification. www.catalystchicago.org/10-01/1001toc.htm

Chicago Teachers Union Quest Center, 222 Merchandise Mart Plaza, Suite 400, Chicago, IL 60654-1016; 312-329-9100; fax: 312-329-6205. www.ctunet.com/quest/

M.A. Smylie, E. Allensworth, R.C. Greenberg, R. Harris, and S. Luppescu. *Teacher Professional Development in Chicago: Supporting Effective Practice.* Chicago: Consortium on Chicago School Research, 2001.

17

Concrete Improvements: Chicago's School Construction Boom

Jacqueline C. Leavy

As executive director of the Neighborhood Capital Budget Group, Jacqueline Leavy has been at the forefront of efforts to promote and improve the school construction and modernization process in the Chicago Public Schools.

Chicago Mayor Richard M. Daley inherited a public school system in 1995 that was in shambles in many respects, including the poor physical condition of the school buildings. In 1993, parents and teachers had already raised the alarm about Chicago's school buildings, spurring the *Chicago Sun Times* to write a series called "Chicago Schools in Ruins," which featured graphic horror stories illustrated with photos of schools that were literally falling apart.

The 1994 U.S. General Accounting Office report on the condition of the nation's public schools cited Chicago as one of the three cities in the U.S. with the worst school facilities.

Clearly, the school buildings in Chicago were a mess. The School Board had no formal capital budget or facilities program because of its perennial budget crises, depending instead upon the Public Building Commission to issue bonds and manage school construction projects. In late 1994, before the mayoral takeover of the Chicago Public Schools (CPS), the "old" Board of Ed finally tried to tackle the facilities crisis, bringing in outside consultants and ranking schools as being in poor, fair, or good condition, or as "in need of replacement." In early 1995, Latino parents who had been seeking overcrowding relief for years went on a hunger strike to get the mayor to release funds to build five new schools.

When Mayor Daley took over the schools, poor building conditions created an immediate, visible way to signal the new era: Fix the school buildings. How better to show that this mayor was determined to remake the public school system, literally from the ground up? And along with mayoral control came political will. The 1995 school reform legislation gave the mayor new flexibility in dealing with the schools' labor unions and finances. His team privatized union jobs, won restrictions on the teachers union bargaining rights, balanced the CPS budget, and—perhaps most importantly— gained a favorable bond rating.

This set the stage for a school construction boom. The new CPS team shelved the old Board's building conditions study and established broad capital spending goals. The initial reaction of parents, students, classroom teachers, and community organizations to the Capital Program was euphoric. Finally, it seemed, problems ignored for years would finally get attention.

CPS moved swiftly to start repairs. Grade school buildings throughout the city had new window systems installed, and asbestos and lead paint were removed. New construction followed. Over the eight years since the mayor took over, CPS has built 19 new schools, 35 additions, and 27 "annexes" (small additions), and is promising to build 15 more schools and ten additions over the next few years.

Perhaps the most striking feature of the CPS school construction program was the speed with which capital funds were assembled and spent. Another important strategy was to conduct *some* repairs, however minor, in as many schools as possible. Since 1996, nearly every school building has been upgraded in some way.

But troubling questions remain to this day: Did CPS address the most urgent needs of the schools? How did CPS choose one project over another? Over time, as reflected in continuing complaints from parents and educators, it appears that too many schools have gotten too little. And systemic issues, such as making improvements needed to deliver curriculum, balancing underutilization and overcrowding, adequately funding maintenance, and openly evaluating the construction process have yet to be addressed. While CPS has made progress in facilities improvements since 1996, there are still serious shortcomings.

One fundamental problem: CPS does not divulge its criteria for ranking the urgency of projects. The public is in the dark about how CPS makes decisions about allocating resources, determining which school gets what improvements, and when. This top-down approach causes communities to question the fairness and timeliness of CPS choices. A community can't be sure when or if its needs will be addressed until its principal is notified that work will begin on a project. While CPS takes testimony at annual school construction public hearings and monthly Board meetings, it provides no rationale for choosing to act or to postpone action on a school's concerns. Projects put on hold, unexplained decisions about who gets overcrowding relief first (or second or third), and last-minute announcements about school closures have all contributed to growing frustration with the CPS construction plan.

Another problem is that the construction plan is not coordinated with neighborhood redevelopment. For example, it does not take into consideration the Chicago Housing Authority "Transformation Plan," or other shifts of school-age populations spurred by residential development and gentrification that are occurring all over the city, especially with the emptying of low-income high-rises. Thus, in the past three years, a new facility "problem" emerged: "surplus" classroom capacity. Declining student enrollment in rapidly changing neighborhoods led CPS to close or consolidate 12 neighborhood schools, with no public input into plans for their preservation, re-use, or alternatives to closure. Another 229 schools have been deemed "underutilized," but CPS has no component in its school construction plan to balance the extremes of underutilized and overcrowded buildings.

One unfortunate result is that old problems seem to be reappearing. It's difficult to measure the extent of remaining health and safety problems, given the lack of detailed information from the Board, but anecdotal evidence abounds. Buildings with leaky pipes, holes in the walls, and overheated, unsanitary cafeterias continue to make headlines. In January 2002, one elementary school roof collapsed into the third-floor gymnasium—miraculously, on a holiday, when no children were present. In July 2003, the *Chicago Tribune* wrote about a West Side school in ruins, with holes in walls and blackboards, no doors on bathroom stalls, and persistent plumbing problems.

In a 2002 survey of classroom teachers, almost half gave their schools a grade of C or lower, and 20 percent judged their school facilities to be educationally inadequate. As the survey revealed, science labs remain a widespread problem. Of the nearly $3.9 billion CPS has allocated so far for school construction and modernization, it has spent just $29 million to renovate science labs in 49 of the city's 96 high schools.

There are a number of other concerns. In general, CPS has focused on elementary schools, barely keeping pace with overcrowding. Meanwhile, 46 percent of Chicago's high school students attend overcrowded buildings. CPS chose to build two small high schools in gentrifying neighborhoods, while in the most overcrowded area of the city parents are still waiting for a new high school. CPS still has no plan to address high school overcrowding, despite the reality that its overcrowded elementary schools must eventually send their 8th graders *somewhere* for high school.

Another unfortunate reality is that communities must almost always mobilize in order to get long-promised or much-needed improvements. Grandparents and parents in Little

Village held a nationally publicized hunger strike in spring 2001 to convince CPS to build a new high school in their densely populated Mexican American neighborhood. It took four years for Northwest Side parents and community groups to win a new building to relieve overcrowding at Kelvyn Park High. In 2002, my organization, the Neighborhood Capital Budget Group, helped organize the community to demand that the city keep its three-year-old promise to replace a crumbling, century-old school building. Once local television stations and newspapers told the story of this forgotten school, CPS allocated $23 million for the new Langston Hughes High School. The Simeon Career Academy was overlooked until 2002, when parents, educators, and neighbors organized to persuade the Board to replace the factory building in which students and teachers had been housed for over three decades.

But in neighborhoods without the capacity to organize, the long wait for better schools continues. Should parents have to resort to hunger strikes and media campaigns to get the school facilities their children need and deserve?

True, CPS could always use more money from the state and federal governments. However, CPS has greater flexibility than virtually any other public school district in the nation to raise capital funds. Its bonding capacity is far from exhausted, and the agency has been able to remain within the property tax cap and still raise enough revenue to cover its debt and meet its budget. The real issue is not money.

Instead, the real remedy is reform of the school construction and modernization planning process itself. Through more equitable and strategic prioritizing, and proactive pursuit of creative financing, CPS could not only use current resources more effectively, but also expand them. The first step would be to create a master plan that publicly ranks facility improvement priorities, addresses health and safety first, and puts facility needs in the context of Chicago's changing neighborhoods. To that end, we are already working with a volunteer citizens' capital planning commission and panel of nationally recognized experts on a proposed Facility Master Plan to equitably and strategically balance Chicago schools' facility needs.

We need a substantive civic dialogue about how to meet the capital needs of our schools, while enhancing the place of our schools in the life of our communities. We need to build educationally appropriate, community-centered, healthy, high-performing facilities to deliver the educational reforms that can transform Chicago's—and our country's—public schools. After all, we are building schools for generations to come. What could be more important?

A Final Word

Ten Questions for Cozette Buckney, Paul Vallas' Right-Hand Woman

Cozette Buckney served as chief academic officer during many of the years that Paul G. Vallas headed the Chicago Public Schools. She now works in the Philadelphia School District as executive assistant for policy and labor relations to Vallas, who became Philadelphia's CEO of schools in 2002. She spoke with editor Alexander Russo shortly before this book went to press.

Russo: What were the Vallas administration's main accomplishments in Chicago?

Buckney: There were three major accomplishments. The first was fiscal stability, being able to run a school system without worrying about funding. Fiscal stability led to union stability, which was number two, because we had contracts, no strikes, we knew that the schools were going to open each year, and people had confidence in the system. And the third was that we had an overarching academic program that addressed the needs of the students.

What was left undone when the Vallas administration was over?

As with anything, there is always room for improvement. The high schools were one of the main areas where we wanted to get more done. We weren't as satisfied as we wanted to be with the improvement rate. We saw the elementary schools getting better and better, but the high schools did not have the same rate of improvement.

What were the most significant obstacles you faced in Chicago?

The biggest obstacle we had was people not believing that we could do it. I think it took about a year, because of [Mayor Richard M. Daley's] constant push in keeping the schools in the forefront and letting people know that all the resources in the city were available for the school district. And it finally made people understand that we could do it.

What were the most significant advantages that you enjoyed?

The biggest advantage we had was having the mayor behind us. No other superintendent had the mayor supporting the school district. The fact that the mayor put his reputation on the line was a major advantage because it was all tied into the city. And having someone who understood that the health and welfare of the city was tied into the health and welfare of the school district was a major advantage.

What, if anything, would you have done differently in Chicago if you had been able to?

I don't think we would have done too much differently, because the conditions of the time dictated so much of what we did. We had a strong, slow, and steady progression that gave people confidence in what we were doing. It showed progress. Now, we could have gone out there in the first year and put everything on the table that we put out over five years, but I don't think that people would have accepted it.

How has that experience helped in Philadelphia?

Because of the experience we had previously and because [we brought with us a team]—people who had been chief education officer, chief of staff, chief financial officer—we were able to come in with a strategic plan and implement it. It clearly has made a difference.

What are the main lessons for other school districts from your experiences in Chicago and Philadelphia?

The main lesson is that, no matter how bad a school system may appear, if you have good people you can do anything. And, most importantly, if you have parents understand that they have an important role in education reform, it can happen.

Do you think that No Child Left Behind is helping urban schools or hurting their progress?

On paper, No Child Left Behind is a fantastic opportunity for school districts to move their achievement plans forward. But in reality, on a year-to-year basis, it is becoming more and more evident that some of the procedures and policies in the plan are just not able to function in a normal school district. For example, the idea of students having the option to transfer out when their school falls below the benchmark is problematic. In some districts, every school fails to meet the criteria, meaning that every single school student in those districts could transfer someplace else. But where would they go? Until you have more schools performing than not performing, this is not really an option.

What more will it take before most middle- and upper-class parents are comfortable enough keeping their children in urban school systems rather than sending them to private schools or moving to the suburbs?

Clearly, keeping middle- and upper-class parents in the school system is one of the goals of any district. You need to have diversity, to have students interacting with all kinds of other students as they grow up. Middle-class and upper-class parents are not going to make the decision to keep their students in a school district unless they feel the school can provide the kind of opportunities they want their child to have. The more a school district can provide those opportunities, whether through magnet schools, special programs, or charter schools, the more people will stay. It is also important to let people know what is happening in their schools—to show them that schools are safe and functioning.

About the Contributors

Alexander Russo, the editor of this volume, is an independent writer and consultant whose writing on education has appeared in the *Washington Monthly*, *Slate.com*, *Education Next*, the *Harvard Education Letter*, and numerous other publications. Russo is a contributing editor for *Catalyst* magazine, based in Chicago, and an associate editor for *The Title I Report*, based in Washington, D.C. He cowrote the 2000 report, *Can Philanthropy Fix Our Schools?* (Thomas B. Fordham Foundation). A regular contributor to Chicago Public Radio's news magazine show, *Eight Forty-Eight*, Russo has also appeared on National Public Radio and WBUR in Boston. His clients have included the National Commission on Entrepreneurship, the Business Roundtable, the National Governors Association, the National Commission on Teaching and America's Future, and the Bill and Melinda Gates Foundation. Between 1993 and 1999, he was an education advisor for California senator Dianne Feinstein, New Mexico senator Jeff Bingaman, and New York City Board of Education chancellor Ramon Cortines. Russo received his master's in education from Harvard University and his bachelor's from Stanford.

John Ayers is executive director of Leadership for Quality Education (LQE), a school reform group that works to bring business resources and ideas to the reform of the Chicago Public Schools. Under Ayers, LQE has focused on principal leadership and the creation of new small schools. He was instrumental in the launching of the city's high-quality charter school initiative in 1996. Before heading LQE, Ayers worked for the Civic Committee of the Commercial Club of Chicago, an economic development group. He also worked for four years in Washington, D.C., as an aide to Illinois congressman Lane Evans. Before that, he spent five years in marketing and sales at the *Chicago Tribune*. He holds an MBA with distinction from Kellogg Graduate School of Management at Northwestern University. Ayers is married to Judi Minter, an early childhood educator, and the couple has two daughters, Dede and Maya. They live in Oak Park, Illinois. Ayers served on a local school council in his neighborhood from 1989 to 1993.

Timothy D. Brandhorst served as the Chicago Public Schools (CPS) director of Labor and Employee Relations and, later, director of Policy Development and Compliance. Before joining CPS he served as an assistant corporation counsel in the Labor Division of the city of Chicago's law department. Brandhorst currently works for the American Bar Association, where he is executive editor of ABA Publishing. He and his wife, Amy, live in Chicago.

Douglas Clayton is director of the Harvard Education Publishing Group, publisher of the award-winning *Harvard Education Letter*, a bimonthly newsletter bridging the gap between practice and research, and the *Harvard Educational Review*, a scholarly journal publishing groundbreaking education research and analysis. HEPG also publishes books for educators, scholars, policymakers, and the general public under the Harvard Education Press imprint. Clayton has taught at Northwestern University and the University of Illinois at Chicago, and he is the former director of the M.A. Program in Publishing and Writing at Emerson College in Boston. He has worked as an editor and administrator at several scholarly, professional, and reference publishers, including serving as Editor-in-Chief at the University of Nebraska Press. Clayton is the author of a biography of the American writer Floyd Dell, and is currently working on a biography of the influential novelist and literary editor, William Dean Howells.

Richard F. Elmore is the Gregory R. Anrig Professor of Educational Leadership at the Harvard Graduate School of Education. His research focuses on the effects of federal, state, and local education policy on schools and classrooms. He is currently exploring how schools of different types and in different policy contexts develop a sense of accountability and the capacity to deliver high-quality instruction. Elmore is a senior research fellow with the Consortium for Policy Research in Education (CPRE), a five-university collaborative engaged in research on state and local education policy and school finance. He is coauthor (with P. Peterson and S. McCarthey) of *Restructuring in the Classroom: Teaching, Learning, and School Organization* (Jossey-Bass, 1996) and coeditor (with Bruce Fuller and Gary Orfield) of *Who Chooses, Who Loses? Culture, Institutions, and the Unequal Effects of School Choice* (Teachers College Press, 1996).

Richard G. Gelb has taught English in the Chicago Public Schools for 22 years. He has been the curriculum coordinator at Benito Juarez Community Academy since 1999. He received his Ph.D. in English (the Language, Literacy, and Rhetoric Program) from the University of Illinois at Chicago in 1999. Gelb has made presentations at national conferences on such diverse literacy/orality practices as verbal art and the practice of Santeria, decoding gang graffiti, poetry via videoconferencing, and a reorientation of high school written composition.

David T. Gordon is the editor of the award-winning *Harvard Education Letter*, a bimonthly publication about K–12 education research and practice written in a jargon-free way for school administrators, teachers, parents, and policymakers. He has edited three books: *The Digital Classroom: How Technology Is Changing the Way We Teach and Learn* (Harvard Education Letter, 2000), *A Nation Reformed? American Education 20 Years after* A Nation at Risk (Harvard Education Press, 2003), and *Better Teaching and Learning in the Digital Classroom* (Harvard Education Press, 2003). In 2003, he won a National Press Club Award for Best Newsletter Journalism.

Philip J. Hansen was the chief accountability officer for the Chicago Public Schools (CPS) from 1997 to 2002. During this time he helped develop and engineer many of the CPS school improvement initiatives targeting the lowest performing schools in Chicago. His office also was responsible for student assessment, teacher accountability, research and evaluation, school quality review, school intervention, compliance, and school improvement planning. Prior to this position, Hansen was a high school teacher, a high school assistant principal, an elementary school principal, a director of special education, and the director of intervention in the Office of Accountability. He is currently on loan to the Illinois State Board of Education (ISBE), where he works with the Chicago Public Schools and ISBE to implement the No Child Left Behind (NCLB) law. He serves as the CPS representative on ISBE's Assessment and Accountability Task Force and the Appeals Advisory Committee, which hears school district appeals relating to their NCLB status. He also consults for the School District of Philadelphia on accountability related issues.

G. Alfred Hess Jr. is the director of the Center for Urban School Policy at Northwestern University and a research professor in the School of Education and Social Policy. Hess has studied the Chicago Public Schools for more than 20 years, starting with a postdoctoral study of desegregation planning by the district in 1980–1981. As executive director of the Chicago Panel on School Policy (1983–1996), a multiethnic coalition of 20 nonprofit organizations, he designed and supervised studies of the district's finances, desegregation efforts, dropout problem, and school-based management reforms, and helped write the 1988 legislation that fostered these latter reforms. Since joining the Northwestern faculty, he has led a three-year multimethods study of high school restructuring and conducted several related studies of high school reform efforts. He is the author of two books on the Chicago reforms: *School Restructuring, Chicago Style* (Corwin, 1991) and *Restructuring Urban Schools: A Chicago Perspective* (Teachers College Press, 1995). In addition to reexamining the district's desegregation efforts after 20 years and advocating for more effective policies to revamp the city's high schools, Hess has been helping small city and suburban school districts examine the achievement patterns of minority students to help them meet the requirements of No Child Left Behind.

Jacqueline C. Leavy has been an advocate for neighborhood revitalization and community empowerment for 29 years. She has served as executive director of the Neighborhood Capital Budget Group (NCBG) for the past 15 years. Leavy helped to build NCBG into a citywide coalition of nearly 200 grassroots community groups and local economic development organizations dedicated to increasing public works in-

vestment and community economic development in Chicago's neighborhoods. Under her leadership, NCBG has become a nationally recognized advocate for rebuilding our urban infrastructure, including public
transportation and public school facilities. Leavy grew up in Chicago,
and prior to coming to NCBG worked for several Chicago-based public
interest organizations and grassroots community groups, including the
Metropolitan Area Housing Alliance, the Northwest Community Organization (in the West Town/Humboldt Park area), Friends of the
Parks, and the Greater Southwest Community Development Corp.
(Chicago Lawn). She holds a bachelor's degree in political science, and
completed three years of postgraduate studies in political science at the
University of Chicago. She also studied urban planning and policy at
the University of Illinois at Chicago.

Linda Lenz is the creator and publisher of *Catalyst: Chicago* and *Catalyst: Cleveland*, monthly newsmagazines that report in depth on the
progress, problems, and politics of school reform in their cities. The
Chicago edition was launched in 1990, the Cleveland edition in 1999
(the publications can be found online at www.catalyst-chicago.org and
www.catalyst-cleveland.org). Previously, Lenz was senior education
writer for the *Chicago Sun-Times* and before that an editorial writer for
the *Chicago Daily News*. After earning a bachelor's degree in journalism from the University of Illinois at Urbana-Champaign, she started
her journalism career as a political writer and columnist for a suburban
Chicago newspaper chain.

Ken Rolling is currently executive director of Parents for Public Schools,
a national organization that engages parents in public school reform,
which has chapters in 15 states. He directed the Chicago Annenberg
Challenge for its entire six-year run, 1995–2002. For ten years before
that, he was associate director of the Woods Fund of Chicago, where he
developed and implemented the Fund's community organizing and
school reform grant programs. Rolling is a board member of the Need-
mor Fund in Toledo, Ohio, and the Shanti Foundation for Peace in
Evanston, Illinois. He is coauthor of a chapter in *Letters to the Next
President: Straight Talk about the Real Crisis in Education* (Teachers

College Press, 2003). He has two grown children who attended Evanston (Ill.) public schools during their K–12 years.

Michael Sadowski is the assistant editor of the *Harvard Education Letter* and the editor of *Adolescents at School: Perspectives on Youth, Identity, and Education* (Harvard Education Press, 2003). A former high school teacher, he is an instructor and an advanced doctoral candidate at the Harvard Graduate School of Education. In 2002, he won a National Press Club Award for Best Newsletter Journalism.

Madeline Talbott is the head organizer for Illinois ACORN, the Association of Community Organizations for Reform Now, an organization of 150,000 low- and moderate-income families organized in 61 cities across the United States. She has been doing community and education organizing with ACORN for 28 years, 20 of them in Chicago. She is a magna cum laude graduate of Harvard University and an instructor in the Masters of Arts in Community Development program at North Park University.

Andrew G. Wade has worked for Chicago school reform for over a decade. Currently, Wade is executive director of the Chicago School Leadership Cooperative, a network of local school councils, neighborhood groups, education organizations, and business leaders united in their support for Chicago's schools. In the early 1990s, Wade served as editor of *Reform Report* for the Chicago Panel on School Policy, where he visited innovative local schools and wrote feature-length analyses of their efforts. In the mid-1990s, Wade was a cofounder of the Chicago Education Network, which provided strategic communications on school reform topics. Prior to getting involved in school reform, Wade worked at the International School of Islamabad, Pakistan, at an alternative school, and as field manager for Minnesota COACT, a network of community organizations. A graduate of Macalester College in St. Paul, Minnesota, Wade is currently pursuing advanced studies in education leadership at the University of Illinois at Chicago. He is married, has a daughter, and resides on Chicago's Northwest Side.

Acknowledgments

First, I want to thank David Gordon of the Harvard Education Press, who gave me the opportunity to work on this book and guided me so skillfully through the process.

Thanks also to the Joyce Foundation, who generously supported the *Harvard Education Letter*'s reporting and writing of some of the articles appearing in this book.

I would like to thank all of those educators, community leaders, advocates, and school reformers who contributed their invaluable thoughts and experiences to these pages. In addition, there are many other school-reform leaders whose advice and expertise have helped me understand (at least partially) the many-layered, multifaceted history of school reform in Chicago.

Thanks also to my friends and colleagues Dan Weissmann, Brett Schaeffer, Tim Brandhorst, and Grant Pick, who have encouraged, advised, and supported me throughout this and many other projects.

Finally, I dedicate this book to my father, a warm and lively presence, a tremendous inspiration, and an educator at heart.